I. D. PERRY

BOB ACTON

A SECON
FR
CARN M RTH

Carn Marth as seen from Trolver Croft (Walk 11). In the foreground is Penpol Creek; Point Quay is in the middle distance, with Restronguet Creek beyond.

Fourteen Round Walks South and West of Truro

A PRACTICAL GUIDE TO A BEAUTIFUL AREA RICH IN HISTORICAL REMAINS

First published 1991

by

LANDFALL PUBLICATIONS

Landfall, Penpol, Devoran, Truro, Cornwall TR3 6NW
Telephone: 0872-862581

A CIP catalogue record for this book is available
from the British Library.

ISBN 1 873443 00 5

I have used this symbol as a visual pun on "Landfall", which is the name of our house, and since the house is near the edge of a low cliff the person who named it was probably making an ironic (or "sick"?) joke of his own. However, there is nothing humorous about the sign when it is used in old mining areas: please keep well clear of places marked in this way. Even where the sign is *not* displayed, for your own safety you should keep to the paths, tracks and roads.

Typesetting, maps and drawings by Bob Acton

Printed by the Troutbeck Press
and bound by R. Booth Ltd.
Antron Hill, Mabe, Penryn, Cornwall

For Katherine and Michael

(Kate and Mike to me)

CONTENTS

Sunset at Carnon Mine (Walk 11)

BOB ACTON

A SECOND VIEW FROM CARN MARTH

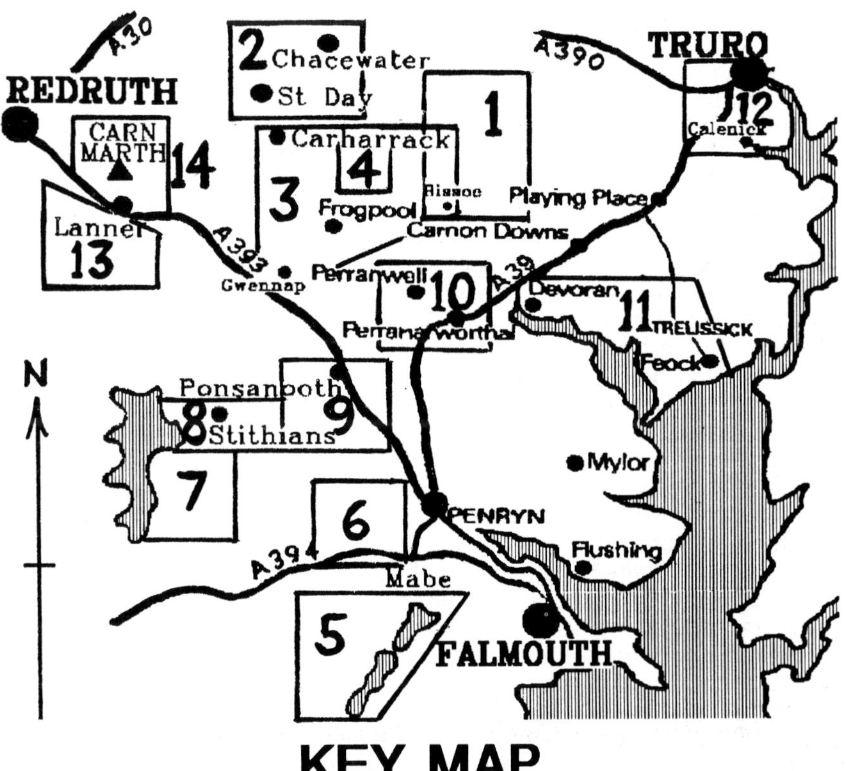

KEY MAP

SKETCH MAP ONLY - NOT TO SCALE

The boxes roughly correspond with the areas covered by the sketch maps for the 14 individual walks.

Together with the detailed directions, the little maps in this book should be adequate to keep you on track, but I strongly recommend you to take with you the relevant Ordnance Survey map, namely No. 203 or 204 in the Landranger series, or ideally one of the larger-scale Pathfinder maps. Most of the routes are on the Truro or the Falmouth and St Mawes sheet, but for the walks around Stithians and Lanner you need Camborne (South) and Camborne (North).

ACKNOWLEDGEMENTS

Among the many delights of writing about local history in Cornwall is the generosity and enthusiasm I encounter everywhere when I seek help and information. In addition to those who gave me valuable assistance with the original *A View from Carn Marth* - namely, Messrs Roy Morton, Peter George, Barrie May and Ivan Corbett - I want to thank the following people: Rose Lewis, the Mineral Tramways Officer, for correcting and updating my item on the Project; Mr A. H. Unwin for information about watermills; Mr Philip Davey, Mr Brian Cock and Mr and Mrs R. J. Wilde for sharing their knowledge of Kea parish with me; Mr John Shields for an update on the Wheal Busy development scheme, plus the history of his house; Mr Allen Buckley for detailed information about the County Adit, and permission to use his map of it, plus much constructive criticism which has enabled me to remove some of the more glaring errors in the original book; Messrs Chris Massie, John Layte, Eric Rabjohns and John Cook for many interesting facts about the Poldice, Goongumpas, Carharrack and Hale Mills area; Mr Alec Wiles for showing my wife and me over Bethel Chapel and telling us about Billy Bray; Mrs Joyce Green for checking through the text of several walks and supplying many details about Stithians; Mr Trevor Edwards of the CTNC for much help and for allowing me to use a map from John R. Smith's *Kennall Vale Archaeological Report;* Mr Bryan Earl for permission to use a drawing from *Cornish Explosives;* Sir William Golding for notes on the history of Tullimaar; Mr Lawrence Butler of Devington's for supplying me with drawings and plans of the proposed development of the Perran Foundry site; Dr Tony Rowland of the Friends of Perran Foundry for checking my note about the foundry; Mr Chris Russell and Mrs J. A. P. Hopkins for information about Lanner; Mr Tony Cartwright for meticulously rereading the whole of *A View from Carn Marth* and making several useful suggestions for corrections and additions; Mr Peter Penpraze, for the reason explained on page 138; and Mr and Mrs J. L. and C. B. Warren of Clifden Farm, Carnon Downs, who buy every book as it comes out, do all the walks, frequently report back, and have pointed out several interesting details in this book which I should otherwise have missed. Above all, I owe a considerable debt to Mr Kenneth Brown of the Trevithick Society, one of the leading authorities on Cornish mining, particularly the design of engines and engine houses, who took immense pains to correct errors in my first draft and contributed many fascinating details. (If I have inadvertently omitted from that long list anyone who ought to have been included, please forgive me.) I'd also like to thank the many local shopkeepers who have not only encouraged me by stocking the books but also kept me informed about recent developments in the locality; I won't name names, because to list them all would take at least another page, and to pick out some might mean a sudden end to my trade with the rest! I am grateful to the Royal Institution of Cornwall for permission to use photographs and other illustrations from its collection, and to *The West Briton* for allowing me to reproduce extracts from articles. Rather than offer thanks here individually to the other writers whose books I have made use of, I have included a list of them at the back, with publication details. Finally, as always I am much indebted to my wife, not only for her active involvement in the walks themselves, the research and the proof-reading, but also for tolerating, usually without much complaint, being left on her own most evenings while I type away at "that *!X?! machine".

INTRODUCTION

It's time for a new edition of *A View from Carn Marth,* and not just because there are only fourteen copies left in stock. Firstly, there were a good many factual errors in the original book which I have been urgently wanting to correct. I am well aware that its successor will probably carry a new crop of mistakes in its turn, but I offer the long lists of books I have consulted, and of experts and local people who have helped me, as evidence that I have tried hard to avoid them. Secondly, there have been dozens of changes during the past couple of years which have a direct bearing on the walks. It's a hopeless task to try to be completely up-to-date, of course: I could go on for ever tinkering with details in the text; but at least I have been able to cover the most important recent developments such as the demise of Wheal Jane. From the point of view of those who enjoy walking, cycling and riding, and who value the legacy of Cornwall's industrial past, one of the most encouraging developments has been the progress made with the Mineral Tramways Project. Thirdly, and most important, I've discovered lots more good walks within the area, all of which are full of historical interest as well as being delightful in themselves. In particular, two very glaring gaps in the original book were the granite-quarrying industry (though of course this was touched on) and the area of Tresavean Mine, very much overlooked by Carn Marth.

I still quite often get asked, "Where *is* Carn Marth?", even by people who live within five miles of it - yet with its quarries at the top and the distinctive engine house on its side it's almost as recognisable as Carn Brea, and the view from the top is even better. The title of my book is based on that of an essay by J. R. Leifchild, "The View from Carn Marth", published in 1857, in which he wrote that "moor and mine, granite and chimneys, steam-engines and *deads,* seem to monopolise the greater portion of the ground from sea to sea. ..... This is one of the very richest portions of England. Right under and around these dead and dreary spots, run marvellous veins of most valuable metal." At that time, the "agriculturist" was almost "completely subdued" by the miner, but now the farmer and nature have reasserted their authority, and the area is one of lush green fields, woods, and moorland clothed in gorse and heather. The evidence that this was once one of the world's most important mining regions is still there, of course, and for me that is what makes it such a rewarding region to explore.

I hope this new book will be one which you will enjoy reading and looking at; but above all I hope that the pictures and the snippets of information will encourage you to go out and see these beautiful and fascinating places for yourself - preferably on foot, of course!

Bob Acton

RIGHTS OF WAY

I have tried hard to ensure that all the recommended routes are on public rights of way, or at least that the landowners have given permission for their use, but it is difficult to be absolutely sure of this, especially in areas of so-called derelict land and around abandoned industrial sites. Please note that the inclusion of any path, track or road in this book cannot in itself confer on readers the right to use it, and that the ultimate responsibility for where you go must be your own. If you do encounter unexpected difficulties on any walk, such as being confronted by impassable barriers, threatening signs or irate landowners, I shall be pleased to be informed about them, and will do my best to investigate the problem and if possible find a way around it - literally or figuratively.

USING THIS BOOK

You will find two types of boxed note in the walks descriptions. Those with heavy outlines contain background information about particular places or features, and these are placed at the relevant point in the directions. An asterisk placed beside a place-name or other word indicates that there is a note about it, usually but not always on the same page. The box with a lighter outline placed at the start of each walk description is designed to be read before you set out: sometimes, in fact, it would be useful to make preparations a day or two in advance in order to get the most out of the walk - for example, you might like to arrange for the key to a church to be available. The introductory notes also give information about driving to the start-and-end point of the walk; parking; how strenuous the walk is likely to be; availability of refreshments and toilets; and any special attractions or other features along the way. It is there that you will find warnings, if required, about such things as unusually glutinous mud, awkward stiles, rickety footbridges and unavoidable stretches of busy road.

Underneath the Key Map on page 5 I have recommended particular O.S. maps for consultation during the walks. Apart from reducing the risk of getting lost, I find that a good map greatly increases the pleasure of a walk by enabling you to put your immediate surroundings into a wider context, and also by encouraging you to make exploratory diversions of your own. The sketch maps in this book are meant simply to complement the written directions, and the numbers shown on them correspond with the numbered sections.

This is by far the largest book I have written, but I trust it will not be too large to fit conveniently into pockets, handbags or map-wallets. As usual, the cover has been laminated to protect it against rain and the effects of being dropped into a puddle. These walks are all quite close to my own home, so I look forward to meeting you on one of them, and hope to see the book in use!

OUTLINE OF THE WALKS

Even for those with no interest in "industrial archaeology" all these walks are delightful in their own right, but my original aim in writing this book was to provide a practical means of understanding the history of mining and related industries in my home area. My imaginary ideal reader, therefore, is one who conscientiously walks all the routes in the order given, reads the relevant boxed note at the place concerned, and then after completing each walk, buys, begs or borrows the other books referred to and goes more deeply into the most interesting details. Just in case this mythical being does actually exist, here is the scheme of the book, showing how I have tried to cover the territory in a logical order.

WALK 1 Introduction to Cornish metal mining: from prehistoric tin-streaming and the earliest underground workings to a modern tin mine.
WALKS 2, 3 & 4 The great mines of Gwennap - for several decades the centre of world production of copper - and the first two mineral railways in Cornwall.

The skyline looking south from Great Wheal Busy (Walk 2)

WALKS 5 & 6 Granite quarrying, which during the 19th century rivalled mining as the leading industry in the Carn Marth / Carnmenellis area.
WALKS 7 - 10 These four walks follow the course of a small river, the Kennall, plus some of its tributaries, from somewhere near its source to its outlet at Restronguet Creek. They provide many examples of the industrial uses of water-power: corn mills, of course, but also paper mills, two gunpowder works and a great foundry which supplied much of the machinery used by the mines.
WALK 11 So now we've reached Restronguet Creek. This walk picks up and develops three of the earlier topics: the recovery of alluvial tin, here actually mined underneath the creek bed; one of the mineral railways again, and the quays it served; and the smelting of some of the ores from the mines.
WALK 12 Apart from exploring part of a later (but still quite early) railway, the walk around Truro takes further the theme of tin smelting, then the "assaying" or testing and selling of the ingots, and finally looks at some of the great town houses built by the families whose wealth came from the mines.
WALK 13 Now we return to the high granite country to see, in contrast to those mansions, the cottages of the miners themselves, to explore the remains of another of the great copper mines and to follow part of a third old mineral railway, all in the shadow of the hill that gives this book its title.
WALK 14 And lastly, the view from Carn Marth, which sums it all up.

Tourism project for mining relics

The West Briton, 30 March 1989

During the summer of 1989, shortly after the original *A View from Carn Marth* was published, the Cornwall Archaeological Unit carried out a programme of research covering a coast-to-coast network linking historic sites in an area centred on Camborne/Redruth. "Dotted with historic buildings, and threaded together by tramroads and railways from north and south coasts, this spectacular but little-known landscape awaits its transformation."(Quoted from the report published in 1990.) Although the disused mineral lines are an important element in the Project, the title "Mineral Tramways Project" is perhaps unfortunate, in that it fails to reflect the huge scope of the enterprise. Its four main aims were and are (as expressed in the report):

* Footpath schemes (both long and short distance).
* The reclamation of Derelict Land (as defined in the County Structure Plan) for amenity.
* The conservation of buildings and other aspects of the Industrial Heritage, both in the wider project area and within the urban centres of Camborne and Redruth.
* The enhancement of local employment opportunities, both directly, as a result of aspects of project implementation, and indirectly, as part of the intended effects of the project on the local economy.

Sponsorship has come from a wide variety of sources: central government, local councils at all levels, national and local industry. The Kerrier Groundwork Trust has been entrusted by the sponsors with the responsibility of co-ordinating work on the project, and a further report, *An Environmental Strategy for Camborne and Redruth,* has been written by Roger Tym & Partners. A tremendous amount has been achieved already: for example, over 60 historic structures have been surveyed as part of the effort to work out an overall strategy for engine-house conservation. In consultation with local experts on mining, such as Kenneth Brown, a start has been made on the reclamation of derelict land and the restoration of those buildings which most urgently need it. The land surrounding mine buildings is often highly toxic and riddled with dangerous shafts, so work has to be done to make it safe, but the Trust is well aware of the danger of "sanitising" these sites: they will not be surrounded by neat lawns and flower beds, but the natural vegetation will return. The Trust is working in close liaison with the CTNC.

Tramway paths into the past

Under this headline in its 17 January 1991 issue, *The West Briton* reported the appointment of Rose Lewis as the Trust's Tramways Project Officer, sponsored by the Countryside Commission and British Telecom. Rose has a special interest in wild life, is widely travelled, and has worked on a similar, though much smaller-scale, project to this one in north-west England.

About a month later, an increase in Government funding for schemes of this sort was announced.

Welcome for derelict land reclamation cash

A conversation I had with Rose just before this book went to press (May 1991) left me feeling very excited about the progress already made and the prospect of so much more. Negotiations concerning several key sites are under way. The focus so far has been mainly on Kerrier, but Carrick seems likely to become more fully involved as work proceeds. The Camborne/Redruth area has been proposed as a World Heritage Site; Rose is convinced that the potential of the areas covered by this book and *A View from Carn Brea* is at least as great as that of sites already designated, such as Ironbridge.

The map below attempts to give some idea of the main routes which will form the basis of the scheme (although Rose stressed that people would be encouraged to use the whole network of paths rather than just the tramway and railway tracks). Some of the mine tramways, such as those serving the Basset Mines and Carn Brea Mine, were too short to be shown on a map of this scale. The former Hayle Railway line between Hayle and Redruth is now, of course, part of the main Penzance - London line, so a route from Camborne to Gwithian using the Red River Valley is planned; but a surprisingly high proportion of the rest of the system shown on the map can still be traced quite easily on the ground, and much of it is already in use as paths, tracks or roads.

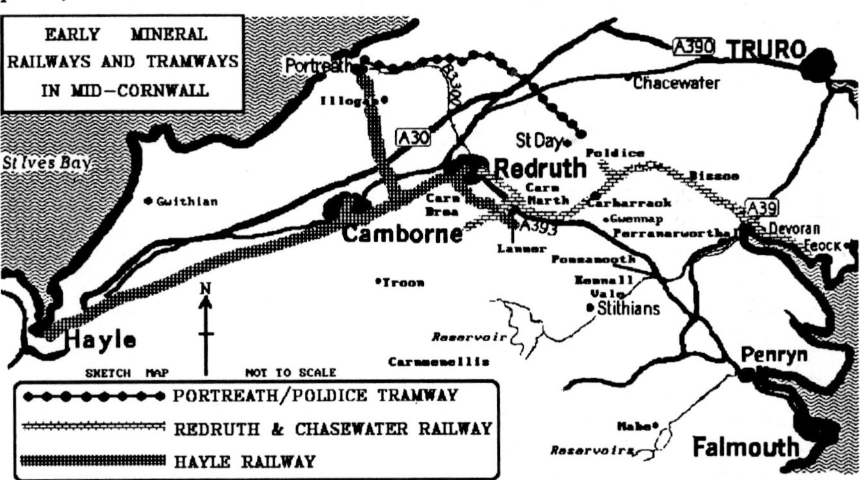

The following sections of the Mineral Tramways routes are included as parts of round walks in *A View from Carn Brea:* most of the Poldice Tramway from Portreath to Wheal Rose; the Incline and some other sections of the Portreath branch of the Hayle Railway; the Basset and Carn Brea Mines tramways; parts of the Red River Valley. *The Landfall Book of the Poldice Valley* looks closely at the tramways and railways of that area; and this book covers most of the Redruth & Chasewater line plus the Tresavean branch of the Hayle Railway: see Walks 2, 3, 4, 11, 13 and 14. On the right is the logo that will be used on the signs.

SOME MINING TERMS

This book is written with the interested general reader in mind, rather than those who have made a special study of mining in Cornwall. Although some explanations of technical terms are included in the main text, I think a brief glossary may prove helpful. Please bear in mind, however, that these are very simplified explanations: several of these words have formed the basis of lengthy articles and even whole books.

ADIT A drainage channel with its mouth or **PORTAL** in a valley or on a hillside or cliff face. In deep mines the water had to be raised by pumping to the level of the adit; this is why statistics often state the depth of a mine "below adit". Adits also often doubled as shafts by following the metal **LODE** (vein), and in some cases provided access for the miners.

BEAM ENGINE Thomas Newcomen of Dartmouth (1663-1729) was the first to develop a steam engine which could be used for pumping water up from the mines. The cylinder was placed vertically, and the piston was chained to one end of a massive wooden or cast iron beam or **BOB** (see the sketch on page 34), pivoted on a strong wall, known as the BOB WALL. The other end overhung the mine shaft and was attached by long rods to the pump at the bottom. In the 1770s James Watt and Matthew Boulton began manufacturing an improved version, and James Pickard modified beam engines to produce rotative motion, used mainly for the **WHIM** (winding) and driving the **STAMPS**. Early in the 19th century, great improvements were brought by the use of high-pressure steam; the research and inventions of Richard Trevithick (1771-1833) made an important contribution here, but many other engineers also played a significant part. The size of each engine was expressed in terms of the diameter of its cylinder: 45", 90", etc.

Killifreth Mine, some time between 1893 and 1897 (see Walk 2). The left- and right-hand engine houses, on Hawke's and Old Sump shafts respectively, were for pumping, and the rocking beams of the engines can be seen projecting from the bob walls. In the middle is the whim engine house, set at right-angles to the other two, so that its bob wall is hidden in this picture. The rotating drum, which is visible, would be used for hoisting and lowering in both the shafts.

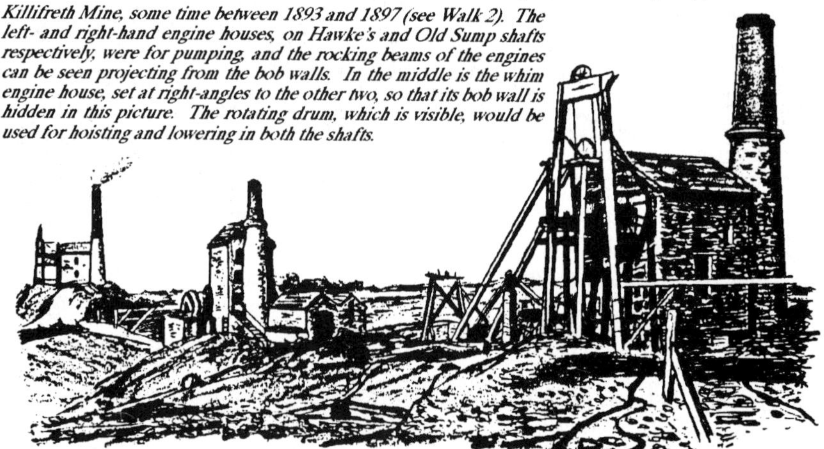

BUDDLE A device for concentrating ore by means of gravity. Early buddles were rectangular, but in the 19th century most were circular; water containing the ore which had been reduced to a fine powder in the stamps was fed into the buddle at the centre or the sides, and rotating brushes were used to ensure that the heaviest, metal-bearing particles settled closest to the inlet point.

BLOWING HOUSE The early form of smelting house, in which the furnace temperature was raised by bellows, usually operated by a waterwheel.

BURNING HOUSE and **CALCINER** (pronounced "cal-*sign*-er") were alternative names for furnaces in which ore was roasted in order to drive off impurities such as arsenic and sulphur. If the arsenic was wanted, the fumes were passed though a long, zigzag flue known as a **LAMBRETH** (labyrinth), from which the deposits were collected.

COUNT HOUSE The mine's office.

DRESSING FLOOR The area where the ore was prepared for smelting.

LEAT An artificial watercourse. Where a leat was carried in a raised trough it was known as a **LAUNDER**. The leat that carried water away from the wheel was called the **TAILRACE**.

SETT "The ground granted to a company of adventurers" (C. C. James) (Adventurers were shareholders in a mining enterprise.) The word "sett" was also used for the granite blocks used to carry rails.

STAMPS Cornish Stamps machines were used to crush the small lumps of ore into material like sand in texture. Heavy timber or iron lifters with iron "heads" at the bottom were raised by cams on a rotating axle, and fell on the ore, fed into a box beneath. Small stamps were usually powered by waterwheels, as in the picture (taken from the Perran Foundry catalogue by courtesy of the Trevithick Society), and larger ones by steam engines.

STREAMING The normal method of winning tin before deep mining became possible. Tin washed down into valleys and buried under silt was exposed, originally by shovel and barrow; the tin-bearing gravel was then sorted and washed, and the waste material used to back-fill the excavated area. Nowadays, earth-movers and lorries do the work.

WHIM A machine for raising water, ore or other heavy materials from the mine. The earliest whims were operated by horses, which walked round and round turning a wooden drum or capstan around which was wound the cable attached to the "kibble" or bucket. Some horse-whims continued in use till the present century, but the whims in deep mines were driven by steam engines, and these were known as "fire whims".

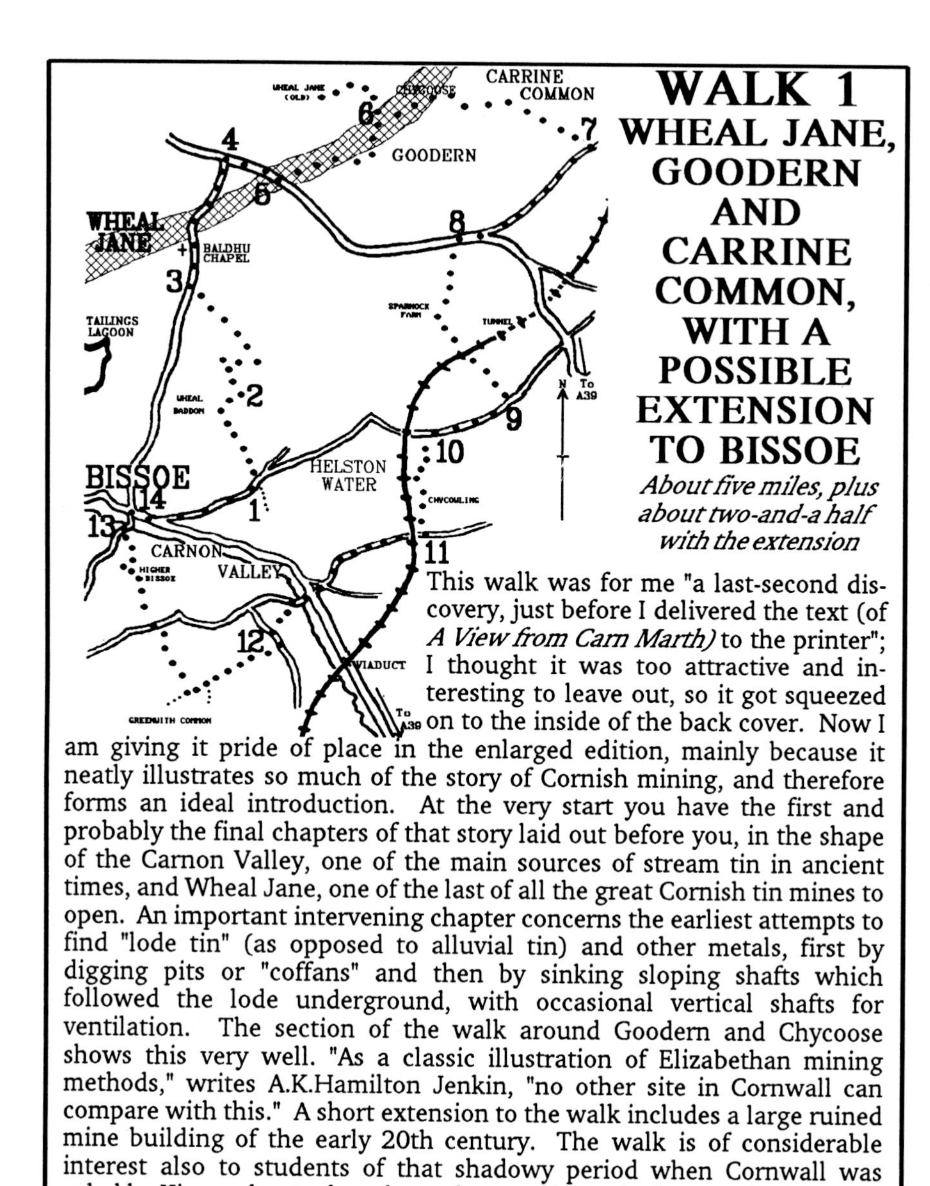

WALK 1
WHEAL JANE, GOODERN AND CARRINE COMMON, WITH A POSSIBLE EXTENSION TO BISSOE

About five miles, plus about two-and-a half with the extension

This walk was for me "a last-second discovery, just before I delivered the text (of *A View from Carn Marth)* to the printer"; I thought it was too attractive and interesting to leave out, so it got squeezed on to the inside of the back cover. Now I am giving it pride of place in the enlarged edition, mainly because it neatly illustrates so much of the story of Cornish mining, and therefore forms an ideal introduction. At the very start you have the first and probably the final chapters of that story laid out before you, in the shape of the Carnon Valley, one of the main sources of stream tin in ancient times, and Wheal Jane, one of the last of all the great Cornish tin mines to open. An important intervening chapter concerns the earliest attempts to find "lode tin" (as opposed to alluvial tin) and other metals, first by digging pits or "coffans" and then by sinking sloping shafts which followed the lode underground, with occasional vertical shafts for ventilation. The section of the walk around Goodern and Chycoose shows this very well. "As a classic illustration of Elizabethan mining methods," writes A.K.Hamilton Jenkin, "no other site in Cornwall can compare with this." A short extension to the walk includes a large ruined mine building of the early 20th century. The walk is of considerable interest also to students of that shadowy period when Cornwall was ruled by Kings, about whom have clustered legends that may be based on historical fact. Again, this is a walk for naturalists: for example, it crosses Carrine Common, an area of open heath which is a valuable wildlife habitat, and passes beside old shafts used by hibernating greater horseshoe bats. Above all, despite an unavoidable few hundred yards on quite a busy road, it is a delightful walk in peaceful countryside. As I write this on returning from it in February 1991, my impression is of sunshine lighting up the snow on every bough and across untrodden fields (colour picture 1), but also of the same lanes in April and May when they are a mass of primroses and bluebells, as described to us by

Mr and Mrs Wilde at Chycoose. In those three months and most others you will probably need waterproof footwear, and if you want food or drink along the way you'll have to take them with you. The extension of the walk down into the Carnon Valley, up on the far side to Higher Bissoe and down to Bissoe Bridge is recommended, but only to those equipped with a good pair of boots, preferably wellingtons.

Finding a parking space for this walk is not easy. At the place where the directions start there is room for a couple of cars to pull off the road, but you may need to seek some other spot where roadside parking is possible. To drive to the start-point from Truro, take the Falmouth road (A39). Continue past Carnon Downs. Just after the main (first) turning to Devoran, turn right towards Bissoe. Continue ahead at the crossroads, under the railway viaduct, and less than a mile beyond that, just before entering Bissoe, turn sharp right uphill on a minor road signposted to Helston Water. After about a quarter of a mile, park on a grassy patch on the right where a track crosses. From here you have a good view of the Carnon Valley and the modern viaduct with the piers of Brunel's viaduct beside it.

1 Take the track on the left, almost opposite the parking place. Ignore the first right turning; just past that is a marshy area with a tip, almost certainly evidence of mining (this area was mined, mainly for lead but also tin, between about 1848 and 1870 by a mine called Great Wheal Baddern, sometimes spelt as Badden or Baddon), and then the main track curves right. At the bend you have a good view of Wheal Jane (*) and its tailings dam (*), with Mount Wellington mine in the distance.

2 At the T-junction turn left on the main track, at the next T-junction turn right, and then at the point where several tracks meet go left, again on the main track. Now you should be heading roughly towards the Wheal Jane building, with a good view over the tailings dam on your left. Ignore the two right turnings: continue ahead to the road.

3 Turn right on that, soon passing Baldhu (*) Wesleyan Chapel. A little way off, to the left, is Baldhu Church; nearby, on both sides, are numerous mineshafts, some capped and others apparently still open. In this part of Cornwall, nearly all the lodes of metalliferous ore run south-west - north-east, and here we have a particularly clear example, because an almost unbroken line of mine workings can be traced from Mount Wellington, through Nangiles and Wheal Jane, and continuing north-east for about another two miles. The next part of this walk will follow the northern part of that line, where the lodes of tin, copper, iron pyrites, silver-lead and zinc, along with plenty of arsenic, some of them deep but others close to the surface, have been exploited at least from Tudor times until the present day. The old shafts and "open-cast entrenchments" as Hamilton Jenkin calls them (MMC Vol.6) close to the chapel are relics of West Wheal Jane (*). Continue along the road, which runs almost due north and therefore soon diverges from the lodes, although you can still clearly see the disturbed ground marking the heavily mined area on the right.

WHEAL JANE

The new Wheal Jane was opened in 1971 after several years' research by Consolidated Gold Fields. The two shafts and the buildings housing the pumps, treatment plant and other machinery occupy the site of old mines, West Wheal Jane and Wheal Widden. Hamilton Jenkin quotes in full the "Articles of covenants and agreements" which Widden's adventurers (shareholders) set out in "Aprill 1684"; he believed these may have been "the first relating to any Cornish company" (MMC Vol.6). The underground workings of Wheal Jane take in the "setts" of several other old mines, such as the original Wheal Jane, further north-east near Goodern, plus Nangiles in the opposite direction; and when Rio Tinto Zinc bought both Wheal Jane and Mount Wellington in 1979 they decided to run them as one unit, thus adding yet more old workings to the modern mine, including parts of Consols and United. Annual production of ore reached 300,000 tonnes in 1984, and by 1985 the main shaft had been sunk to 514m. The grade of tin was low compared to South Crofty's, but copper, zinc, wolfram, arsenic and fluorspar were also produced. In October 1985 the price of tin dropped to £3,300 per tonne, having been as high as £10,500 a few months earlier. Government loans kept Wheal Jane alive then, but that was far from being the end of the story, as is shown by these two extracts from articles in the *West Briton.* The first was published on 16th February 1989.

New hope as tin price rises

ELEVEN months after the management buy-out of the Wheal Jane and South Crofty mines there are strong signs that they are on target for making the operation profitable.

Although there is still a long way for the Carnon Consolidated operation to go, recent increases in world prices for metals and change in the value of the pound have helped bring the break-even figure for tin production within striking distance.

When the managers bought the mines from RTZ last year, the prices per ton of its three main products were tin £3.784 zinc £497 and copper £1,324.

This week tin had risen to £4,449, zinc to £1,034 and copper to £1,648.

Mr. Brian Calver, managing director of the company, said he was still cautiously optimistic that they would succeed in bringing the mine to profit, and was beginning to feel more and more confident that it would happen.

But that confidence was misplaced.....

£35m scheme to transform Wheal Jane

PLANS to transform the Wheal Jane tin mine at Baldhu, near Truro, into a massive £35-million leisure, tourist and business complex have been unveiled.

Mine owners Carnon Consolidated said the ambitious scheme would mean 450 new jobs and a £22 million-a-year boost for the local economy. Another 200 jobs would be created indirectly.

The aim is to restore the 360-acre site of Wheal Jane and the Carnon Valley, where mining ends next year, and give the company stability to safeguard Cornwall's last working tin mine at South Crofty.

Key features

Key features, which Carnon predict will attract more than a quarter of a million visitors a year, include

★ championship 18-hole golf course with golf academy, country club, squash and tennis courts

★ 100 bedroom health hydro

★ 230 golf and holiday lodges with 60 staff homes

★ a mining trail for visitors including a trip 200 feet underground

★ a commercial glasshouse operation growing tomatoes, peppers and exotic plants

★ a themed pub and restaurant

★ business park with 2,500 square meters of accommodation

★ butterfly farm

★ restoration and landscaping of the Carnon Valley with footpaths and tramways open for walkers, riders and cyclists

The company said the project would mean the "greening" of many acres of derelict mining land in line with Government policies for the environment.

Energy

Hot water pumped from the mine would be used as a renewable source of energy for the glasshouse operation. And continued pumping would enable mining to be restarted if the incustry's economy recovered.

(15th November 1990)

This ambitious scheme has the backing of the Bissoe Valley Residents Association; but whether it will materialise, and how it will affect the walks in this book, remains to be seen. By March 1991 the plan to offer underground visits had been abandoned (except possibly at the shallowest levels) because Government aid was suddenly cut off and the workings were allowed to flood.

TAILINGS DAM

In a modern metal mine, when all the valuable minerals have, as far as possible, been removed from the ore, water containing the fine particles of waste material is piped into a dam. There they gradually sink to the bottom, and the water is returned to the mine for re-use. Eventually, when the tailings filled the reservoir and dried out, the area would in theory be landscaped and grassed over; in practice, however, some tin and other minerals still remain, and with improved technology the tailings may be re-worked if prices justify it.

BALDHU

It means "black mine", although Oliver Padel suggests that "bal" would more accurately be translated as "an area where surface working was carried out, perhaps a group of workings". The oldest documented use of the word was in fact in the phrase *bal dew,* in 1593. Like St Day and Chacewater, it became a separate parish in the first half of the 19th century, when the populations of nearby villages such as Twelveheads and Bissoe were greatly swollen by the success of the mines; and like St Day Church, Baldhu Parish Church is now disused. Not quite visible from this walk is the so-called Three Eyes(#)chapel at Kerley Downs, one of three built by Billy Bray. (See the note on Billy Bray and his Chapels, Walk 4.) Roger and Esther Race's *Hidden Cornwall* (privately published in 1982) tells the story of the Rev. W.Haslam, the first vicar of Baldhu, and his relationship with Billy Bray. At first Haslam was suspicious of the Methodists; later, he was "converted in his pulpit", and when Billy discovered this, "he picked him up, ran him round the room and then rolled all over the floor, for sheer joy! Then they all had breakfast." Billy's grave, surmounted by an impressive memorial, is close to the church's south door; the grave is lovingly tended, with a vase of artificial flowers still intact despite recent gales, whereas the church is boarded up and deserted. I regret not having been able to fit the church and chapel into a round walk: they certainly deserve a visit.

(#)"Our little chapel had three windows, one on one side, and two on the other; the old devil, who does not like chapels, put his servants by way of reproach to call our chapel *Three-eyes.* But, blessed be God, since then, the chapel has become too small for the place, and it has been enlarged; now there are six windows instead of three; and they may call the chapel *Six-eyes* now if they will." (Quoted in BBKS.)

WEST WHEAL JANE

Originally known as Baldhu, this mine was said in 1819 to have "commenced at a period so remote that no memorials of the time are preserved." In 1860 it employed 200 people, producing mainly iron pyrites; although its fortunes declined sharply after that, the shallower workings continued to be exploited for tin at least till 1919. From 1905 to about 1915 it was attached to a group called Falmouth Consolidated Mines; from 1939 till 1941 it belonged to the Mount Wellington group; and since 1971 it has been the site of the modern Wheal Jane.

4 At the main road, turn right. PLEASE TAKE CARE: THIS IS QUITE A BUSY ROAD, SO WALK FACING THE ONCOMING TRAFFIC AND USE THE VERGE WHERE POSSIBLE.

5 After about a quarter of a mile, turn left on to a wide track (the second track on that side), and now once again you are following the lodes. This section, as I mentioned in the introductory note, shows particularly clear evidence of having been worked by "old men" (that is, before written records began to be kept, late in the 18th century), but from about 1740 it was known as Wheal Jane. Collins in OWEMR records that "in 1870 it was 180 fathoms deep (on the very flat lode) and employed 300 people." Like West Wheal Jane, it seems to have stopped work in the mid-1870s, apart from small-scale operations at the shallower levels, until the re-opening described in section 6. At first there are several shafts on the left, and then quite deep caverns on the right, especially beyond the buildings of Goodern Manor Farm (*). (The village on the skyline to the left, by the way, is Threemilestone.)

GOODERN MANOR

Goodern Manor is listed in the Domesday Book under the name "Woderon"; at that time it had 60 acres of woodland, but it is (to quote Charles Henderson) "now comparatively treeless owing to the mines." (ECH) He also points out, however, that there are still woods at Nansavallan and Killiow, which were then parts of the Manor. On and around Goodern Manor Farm on the OS maps there is a cluster of words in the Old English script indicating ancient sites: "Earthwork" or "Settlement" and "Tumulus" close to the farm buildings, and at least four other tumuli to east, south and west. As I said in my introductory note, legends tend to gather around such places, and they find their way into print in such passages as this, from Joy Wilson's *Cornwall, Land of Legend* (Bossiney, 1989): "old documents speak of this place (Goodern) as having been once a 'castle' of irascible King Teudar who here fought a battle against Christians. During the battle he was killed by a fall from his horse, and is thought to have been buried beneath a large tree-crowned barrow that stands close by. Teudar's Christian successor King Mark

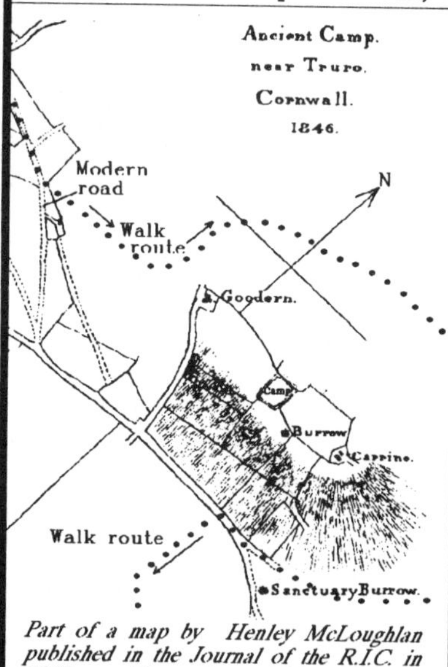

Part of a map by Henley McLoughlan published in the Journal of the R.I.C. in 1847 - with a few additions by me. "Sanctuary Barrow is where the Midsummer Fires were lit" according to W.H.Pascoe.

is thought to have used Goodern as a hunting lodge." Thus some writers about Tristram and Iseult (Tristan and Isolda) conclude that Goodern was Iseult's destination when her lover, disguised as a leper, carried her across the ford at Malpas. ("Perhaps in those earlier times the Truro River was shallower," speculates Mrs Wilson, and similarly she adds to her comments about Goodern, "And in the level meadow alongside perhaps the tournament and Iseult's Ordeal witnessed by the kings was staged.") The suggestion that Goodern Manor was once an administrative centre gains some support from the closeness of Helston Water: Cornish, *hen-lys,* "ancient court", plus Old English *tun,* "manorial centre", and from the fact that this area was once called Alba Landa or Blancheland, which is the setting of King Mark's hunting lodge in the Tristan story. Early references to Goodern as a palace of King Teudar include the Cornish episode in the play of *The Life of Meriasek,* probably written by a cleric at Glasney College (see Walk 5) early in the 16th century, and the Breton *Life of St Kea* (1636), in which it is called Gudrun; I called them "early references", but they were both written about a thousand years after King Teudar's time. For more detail, see TKC, especially pages 24-5, 41 and 58. Other stories possibly based on fact have attached themselves to Goodern and its immediate surroundings: Mrs Wilson writes of the farmer in Tudor times who "dug up at Goodern - within the enclosure - enough gold and silver to transform him from peasant to gentleman." Maybe this is in essence the same story that Sheila Bird mentions in BCV: "An old legend told of a crock of gold found beneath the old cross, which was removed from the finder's possession by the landowner, who thereafter was unable to keep stock on his land, unless the animals were branded with the protective sign of the cross keys." The "old cross" has never been identified, but references exist to "Kea wayside cross", and that hardly suggests that it was located inside the earthwork. According to LPH, the crock of gold was found by a labourer living at Goodern, and the farmer who appropriated it was "the possessor of Goodern". The medieval Manor House was rebuilt about 1605, and the Tudor house was burnt down late last century, apart from one section incorporated in the existing building. Although there is so little nowadays that the casual passer-by would notice of the ancient sites at Goodern, the place still exerts a hold on people's imagination: we heard about the residents of a house nearby a few years back who went and prayed at the earthwork every morning. As for "Blancheland" (or "Blanchland") - no-one knows for sure why the Kea area should have been given this name. One suggestion is that a certain type of white stone is common there, but I prefer Philip Davey's theory, that hawthorn is unusually prolific in the area, and (unsurprisingly) I like my own notion best of all: I don't know how many orchards are still at Nansavallan, but have you been to Coombe when the Kea plum and apple trees are in blossom?

The remains of the power house of the old Wheal Jane

6 Soon after the farm, for the main walk route keep to the main track as it bears right, *but I recommend a short diversion along the track ahead. Soon on the left is a capped shaft beside which rest two huge granite blocks; just what these were used for is doubtful. The track becomes a woodland path. At the clearing, keep on the upper path as it curves left, and it brings you to one of the largest ruined mine buildings in mid-Cornwall, the power house built in 1907 when Wheal Jane was re-opened as part of Falmouth Consolidated Mines. The chapel-like structure, with its "Norman" arches and circular window, is rather reminiscent of the beautiful buidings at Marriott's Shaft, South Wheal Frances (see* A View from Carn Brea, *Walk 10). The trees growing inside (colour picture 2) lend it an air of mystery and charm which is rudely shattered by comparing a photograph of the interior in 1908 showing the ore-crushing machinery in place: MC photograph 65. Just as surprising is the preceding picture, showing the rest of the buildings as they were then, with the upper part of the power house just visible on the left. The ruins of many of the other buildings are still there, Giles's Shaft is at the top of the slope above the power house, and a short way below the buildings is a large waste-dump (called "sands" or a "burrow" in Cornwall). Return towards Goodern by the same route, turning left when you get back to the main track.* After a short distance, don't miss the mineshaft on the left, called Tremayne Shaft, boarded over but still issuing fumes early in 1991, showing that it was linked to the workings of the modern mine. We were told that in recent years it was sometimes used for underground visits by students at the Camborne School of Mines. On the south side of it are the remains of a stone crusher station. The cottage on the left soon after this is Chycoose, "the house in the woods". Mr and Mrs Wilde, who live there, told us that beneath their land is "an underground river" (perhaps an adit?), and caves or shafts used by greater horseshoe bats. (A BBC TV crew spent two or three days filming them in 1990.) It is also said that a type of luminous moss grows there. The track on the left beside Chycoose was cleared a few years ago by Wheal Jane, who opened up a shaft near the valley bottom, where there are also various old mine adits. In the valley are the main London-Penzance railway line and the stream that meets the Truro River at Calenick. Mr Brian Cock, who farms Goodern, told me that the stream is known as the "River Tinny". The main track now leaves mining country, and once past the house called Fenton Goose ("fountain or spring in the woods") you are soon crossing Carrine Common (*), with panoramic views of the south-western edge of Truro, dominated (from left to right) by Treliske Hospital, Richard Lander comprehensive school, and New County Hall. Keep to the main track, curving right, which eventually brings you to a road. (There are several side-tracks and paths which are pleasant to explore and obviously much-used, but not official rights of way.)

CARRINE COMMON

We were first attracted to this spot about three years ago after hearing a Radio Cornwall programme about its interesting flora and fauna. It is described in NC as "a comparatively small area of dry heathland with a good growth of Dorset Heath - this species normally thrives in much wetter conditions." The name, which means "cold fort or round", may relate to the earthwork at Goodern. It is pronounced "Careen" , but local people, or at least some of them, refer to the Common as "Cryon Downs", and there is a legend that it got its name from the "crying" of the mothers, widows and sweethearts of those killed in the great battle between King Teudar and the Christians: see the note about Goodern. It is also firmly believed by many that the ghost of a headless woman stalks the tracks and paths on the Common; it was seen by "Mistress Sarah" of Carrine Farm, who was struck blind - though how long afterwards that happened we were not told.

7 Turn right at the road, and after nearly half a mile right again at the main road, which again "craves wary walking".

8 Take the first left turning, the minor road leading to Sparnock ("thorntree") Farm. Immediately past the farmhouse, go through the six-bar metal gate on the left, and walk straight ahead along a rough, muddy track created mainly by tractor-tyres. This leads to a five-bar wooden gate, beyond which is a bridge over the Falmouth branch line, with a tunnel on the left, and then a narrow woodland path which could easily become overgrown, although we met with no problems in March 1989 or February 1991. At the field, continue ahead (despite the waymark arrow on the wooden post) with the hedge on your right and through a metal gate to another road.

9 Turn right on that. It slopes gently downhill for about half a mile.

10 Just before you reach the railway bridge, if you want to extend the walk to the other side of the Carnon Valley turn left at a lane with signs naming Kestrel Cottage and Halleggo ("willow-trees") Farm; continue reading the directions that follow the lines in italics. *To return direct to the starting-point, continue down the road, passing under the railway before reaching a stream flowing south to join the Carnon River; the road then climbs past a cottage whose name shows it once housed a blacksmith's workshop - this is at Helston (or Helstone) Water: see the note about Goodern - and soon you are back where you started.* To continue the extended walk, fork right at the signs "Hannam" and SGBawden". This leads down to another railway bridge (notice the good view of Carn Marth, almost straight ahead), but just before you reach the bridge turn left on to a pretty but very muddy (I did warn you!) woodland lane. Before reaching the road this becomes a path.

11 Turn right at the road, which passes under yet another railway bridge and slopes down quite steeply through attractive countryside to a ford with a footbridge consisting of two long granite blocks which illustrate very well the method by which they were split: see the photographs on page 16 of Q&Q. (The ford is called Dunstan's Ford, so I wouldn't be surprised if some keen Tristan-hunter has speculated that Tristan carried Isolda across here rather than at Malpas: was Dunstan really Drustanus.... or just a local farmer?) Next comes a very boggy area on the left. At the main road, continue ahead across the flat valley-bottom. *Just before the bridge over the Carnon River you could shorten the walk by using the track on the right, which would bring you quite quickly to Bissoe Bridge; turn right on the road there and pick up the directions at point 13, line 5.* For the longer (and muddier) route, cross the bridge and immediately turn left on a narrow path with a sign to Grenna and Frogpool. Go up a few steps, through a small gate, and then you have a steep climb, keeping beside the hedge on your right. From here there are good views of Wheal Jane on the skyline to the right, the viaduct on the left and the valley behind. Pause for a moment and reflect on how much this place has changed. "The broad Carnan or Devoran Valley, " writes Henderson in ECH, "now mine-scarred and sterile, must once have been very well wooded, to judge from its place-names." The woods presumably swept right down to the banks of what was until at least medieval times a navigable river.

12 At the minor road, turn left, then first right along a surfaced road which after Tregew ("farm of the hollow") becomes a track. Ignore the track on the right after about a quarter of a mile; where the main track curves left continue ahead for about a hundred yards, then cross the stile in the hedge on the right. Walk with the hedge on your left at first, but where that curves left continue straight on down this long field to the gate at the far right-hand corner. In February 1991 this field had been ploughed and planted, and there was no sign that any attempt had been made to re-instate the footpath, so you may have to walk through the crop; please take care to do as little damage as possible. At the road, go a few feet to the left, then turn right on the track to Higher Bissoe, where you go through a wooden gate, among buildings, and join a gravelled drive that slopes down to another road.

13 Turn right and cross Bissoe Bridge (*), from which you can look left to a small waterfall at the eastern end of a site now managed by the Cornwall

The Carnon Valley, about 1908. On the left can be seen the track of the Redruth and Chasewater Railway.(Courtesy R.I.C.)

BISSOE BRIDGE

Bissoe is one of the names Henderson must have had in mind when he wrote the comment I quoted near the end of section 11: it means "birch trees". The bridge looks old, but whether it is actually the bridge that stood here when Bissoe Bridge marked the upper limit of navigation and Bissoe was the port for the mines of Gwennap, I don't know. D.B.Barton in ECMH Vol.2 writes, "Certainly, the tide once ebbed and flowed to the Bissoe we know today but with the passage of time and with silting - itself a process greatly accelerated by streaming - the tidal limits withdrew steadily seawards." C.C.James thought that "at a remote period" the tide maight have reached "Cusgarne and beyond," and he states, "In 1620 boats up to 200 tons burthen came up to Bissoe Bridge." (HPG). The birches must have been victims many centuries ago, not only of the tin streamers themselves but of many other industries that would have been attracted to the spot when sea-going boats could reach it; and even long after the tidal waters had departed and the railway had arrived Bissoe remained an industrial centre, with watermills, smelting works, arsenic refineries, paint factories, chemical plants (including ochre and vitriol works), hardcore works, tin-dressing floors and various other enterprises at various times; today a concrete manufactory stands near the bridge, and there is talk of drilling into hot rocks near Point Mills (see Walk 3). The industrial history of Bissoe is clearly far from complete; but if I have made it sound like Cornwall's Black Country I have done it a disservice, because it has a special attraction of its own, and is a place I always enjoy visiting.

Trust for Nature Conservation, and beyond that to the sad remains of what was until very recently the tall, graceful arsenic works stack. (See Walk 3.) The road passes among typical miners' cottages. A lean-to shed at Hazel Cottage is named Railway Villa in recognition of the fact that the lane on the right immediately beyond the cottage is the trackbed of the Redruth and Chasewater (see Walk 3 again); some granite setts (sleeper-blocks) are among the stones that have been used to make a rough wall on the left.

14 Turn right on the main road. It's usually busy, so use the pavement and later the verge on the right. Fork left up the road signed to Helston Water to return to the starting-point.

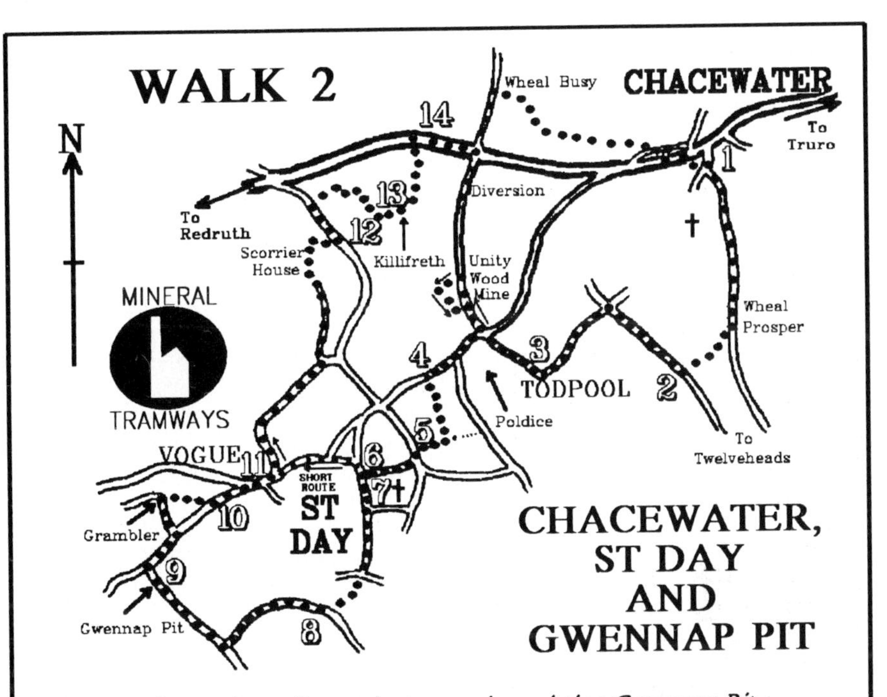

About nine miles, or just over six omitting Gwennap Pit

Here is a walk in the heart of copper-mining country, very rich in relics of Cornwall's industrial past and yet passing through much attractive countryside. Scorrier is on the route of Cornwall's oldest railway, which linked some of the mines on the walk to the north-coast harbour of Portreath. If you have the time and strength to do the full nine-mile walk, you can see Gwennap Pit, where Wesley preached so often to the miners and their families. The areas around Poldice and Great Wheal Busy are heavily scarred by industry, but in contrast the walk includes an attractive valley, several stretches of pleasant, open countryside, and some beautiful woodland. The bulk of the walking is on quiet, minor roads and well-made tracks, so mud underfoot should not be a problem. Vogue, Chacewater and St Day all have well-recommended pubs, and the last two also have shops and public toilets.

To drive to Chacewater from Truro, take the A390 westwards; after about three miles turn left at the Threemilestone roundabout, signposted Chacewater. For the car park, turn left in the centre of the village, just past the King's Head.

1 Turn left at the car park entrance and take the minor road signposted to Twelveheads. Walk down this attractive valley (see note on Wheal Prosper) for just over half a mile, and then turn up the rough track on the right, which comes shortly before a minor road on the right. The track takes you past Chy Mengleth, complete with its bus-stop sign and a notice proclaiming, "Penalty for NOT shutting gate £2", on a gate securely fixed open.

Chacewater Church

WHEAL PROSPER

The valley feels very rural, and its "industries" now consist of such things as smallholdings and a vineyard, but just a few yards past the point where we turn up to the right is a modern water-wheel, reminding us of how industry once exploited most of Cornwall's streams; and up on the left was once Wheal Prosper, one of several Cornish mines given that hopeful name. Unfortunately, this one was never a great success, and didn't work except in a very small way after 1840. Now it is difficult to find any trace except some dumps and its name on the maps. On the site of what is now a herb farm was "Tippett's Stamps", referring to a Cornish Stamps machine for crushing tin ore: see the note on Twelveheads in Walk 3.

2 At the road, turn right. On the skyline to the left are at least three old engine-houses belonging to the great United and Consolidated copper mines, plus the base of the "Consols" clock tower (on Walk 3). After you pass Wheal Henry farm there are mining remains close by on the right. Most of Wheal Henry's workings were on the valley-slopes just south of here; it was a tin-and-copper mine made up of several ancient small ones with optimistic names like Goodluck and Come-to-Good (compare Prosper). See PV for fuller details and a map of the old workings dating from 1837. Continue for nearly half a mile till you reach a crossroads. Here you turn left. The elegant engine-house chimney on the right is Killifreth. The woods beyond are around Scorrier House. St Day is on the hilltop. You are now approaching an area of very intensive mining, mainly of copper and arsenic; Poldice mine is straight ahead on the far side of the upper Carnon Valley, which has been scoured for minerals time out of mind and now at a casual glance resembles the proverbial moonscape, but you should see it when the heather's in full bloom! Again see Walk 3 and PV for fuller details.

TODPOOL

Todpool (perhaps meaning "pasture-land beside the pool") in the nineteenth century was a thriving mining community with its own pub - now No. 8 on the right near the corner. There are several good examples of the tiny cottages many miners lived in. On their doorstep were at least three important mines: Poldice, Wheal Unity and Creegbrawse.

3 At Todpool (*), where the road turns right for St Day, continue ahead past the Todpool Gate sign erected in 1990 by the Poldice Valley Trust. The valley had suffered a long period of neglect and mistreatment, and the Trust was formed (to quote its Chairman, D.H.Lanyon) "with the aims of preserving and where necessary restoring the valley landscape and heritage." Below is an extract from an article published in *The West Briton* on 14 February 1991.

Restoring the valley's pride

WORK on restoring derelict land in the Poldice Valley, near St. Day, is now under way as a result of donations totalling £3,000 from local companies and organisations and the promise of £1,000 from Carrick Council.

People living in the vicinity, concerned about the valley's future, formed a trust at the beginning of last year. Their aim is to help the scarred landscape recover and to open up the valley for walkers, cyclists and horse-riders.

They also see it as a valuable resource for schools in the area, as well as an important wildlife habitat in urgent need of protection and conservation.

There is a great deal to see in this area, but for now I suggest just a quick look at the remains of the arsenic works on the site of Poldice Mine (*), which are far more interesting than they may look from a distance, and seem to me to have the air of a ruined castle. When you are ready to go on, return to the road and turn left. Continue to the next crossroads. Here you could turn left for St Day, but it is well worth going straight on to see the two fine engine houses at Wheal Bush Farm, which were part of Unity Wood Mine (*). When you reach them, go down the track on the left, from which you can approach the left-hand (pumping) engine house. Continue down this track and then take the next one on the left. This brings you back to the crossroads, where you turn right for St Day. Ignore the left fork in the road.

POLDICE MINE (Colour picture 6)

Thomas Tonkin, writing early in the 18th century, referred to Poldice as "this famous work, which is esteemed to be the deepest in the county, being 106 fms", and explained "dice" as a corruption of (St) Day's. First it was worked mainly for tin, but later became an important copper mine, without ever quite recapturing the pre-eminence it had had as a tin mine. Much of what remains now reflects its final phases of activity, arsenic production and the treatment of ore from Park-an-Chy Mine, St Day. Several round buddles, used to separate metal from waste matter by gravity, are clearly visible: for more about buddles and much more about Poldice, see.... Well, I'll leave you to guess which of my other books.

UNITY WOOD MINE (Colour pictures 6 and 7)

Unity Wood Mine apparently opened in 1815: that, at least, is the date of the earliest figures quoted. It was quite a productive copper mine and also raised some tin, but like so many other Cornish mines it suffered in the late 1860s and early 1870s because of competition from abroad, especially South American copper and Australian tin. It closed in 1873, but under the names of West Poldice and Tolgullow United re-opened at various times up to 1903. It took its original name from the wood just to the west, which in turn took its name from Wheal Unity, near Todpool hamlet; before that the wood was called Killifreth ("speckled grove").

4 Shortly after the fork, turn left on to the public footpath signposted to Crofthandy. (The used-car dump on the left is a sample of modern industry for comparison!) Just after the dump, fork right (look for a waymark arrow on a post on a mound among the heather), then go straight on past two houses on your left, and along a lane. The short stretch of path you have just come along, since leaving the road, follows the course of the Poldice/Portreath Tramway: see the later note about Scorrier House. At the crossroads (Kernyk), turn right, and when the main track bears right continue along the narrower path straight ahead.

5 At the road turn left, past Pine Cottage, and then at the crossroads turn right into St Day (*).

6 When you reach the T-junction, you have the choice of continuing to Gwennap Pit, or returning to Chacewater by a route nearly three miles shorter. For the latter turn right, then left almost immediately, following the Redruth signs. After passing the clock tower (toilets here) and St Day Inn, ignore the next two right turnings, continue down Vogue Hill and take the narrow road on the right, Pink Moors. Now continue following the directions from Point 11. For Gwennap Pit, turn left at the T-junction, passing the remains of the old church on your left.

7 Where the main road bends left, go straight on along a minor road, past the school. At the T-junction (wooden fencing), cross to the path opposite. Soon it turns into a small road. Where it bends left by a pair of old cottages, go right and continue to the road.

8 Turn right. Now you have a good view of St Day and the Carnon Valley to the right; you also pass some attractive old houses, including Trevethan ("farm of the little grave") House, with its old farmhouse and grain-store. Continue uphill and follow the road round to the right, signposted "Gwennap Pit". Before you reach it you will see the remains of Cathedral Mine's engine-house on the left. This mine was the scene of an underground flood which killed five men and three boys in 1881; the story is told in CMD (pages 85-6).

9 After about half a mile, Gwennap Pit (*) is clearly signposted to the left. Cards, booklets and other "souvenirs" can be obtained at the new chapel on the right before you enter the pit; if this is closed, cross to the far side of the pit to the exit gate, and call at the house on the right. To continue the walk, return to the main entrance, turn left at the road and right at the T-junction,

ST DAY

"The only visitors that ever come to St Day," a customer in a grocer's shop told me, "are lost, looking for the A30." According to the owner of the shop, "There isn't a miner left in the village now." If that seems surprising, remember how short the average life-span of a miner was, and also how many of the younger men emigrated to new mining enterprises abroad when the Cornish industry declined. An excellent symbol of the change in St Day's fortunes since the days when it boasted nine pubs is the "old" church .... not so very old, because it was built in 1828. At that time St Day was known as "the mining capital of Cornwall", and a church big enough to seat two thousand was essential. (In 1841 Gwennap parish had a population of 10,800, more than any other except Madron, which included the whole of Penzance.) Now the church is a sad ruin: it was condemned as unsafe in 1956; part of the roof fell in in 1985 after vandals broke in and removed a pillar, with the result that the rest of the roof had to be dynamited as a safety measure; and the famous "Gothick" tower will inevitably suffer a similar fate before very long unless local efforts to raise a large sum for restoration bear fruit. Pevsner in his book on Cornwall remarks that St Day Church "looks over a landscape of deserted mines, like so many monuments to the passing of human achievement, more deeply moving than the artificial picturesque mementos in 18th century gardens." The hall opposite, which serves as the church now, has an interesting collection of photographs of old St Day. A little booklet about the new church also gives a few details about the sixth century monk who founded the original Trinity Chapel here, and mentions how it became an important shrine attracting many pilgrims. The St Day Feast is held on the third Monday after Whit each year: there are parades led by the local band, and a dance; traditionally, the youngest children receive a saffron bun, older ones a shilling (50p now), and the old-age pensioners have a tea-party. St Day, twice referred to by Polsue as "a pretty little town" (LPH), is well worth exploring for the Georgian and Victorian houses and shop-fronts; a series of photographs published in a recent *West Briton* supplement ("Down the Years", 21 February 1991: well worth seeking out) showed just how little most of the buildings in the centre have changed during the last century. The granite clock tower, which has recently been renovated, was erected at a cost of £400 in 1821 (1831 according to Polsue). The wooden structure at the top was removed to St Day from the rather similar clock tower in Redruth about 1905 - at what cost I don't know.

passing Trenarth ("farm of the height") on your right. After about a quarter of a mile you will reach Mynheer Farm. Like Tremenhere (Walks 8 and 9), its name refers to an ancient longstone. Perhaps in this case the allusion is to the Roman milestone ploughed up here in 1942: some details are given on a wall plaque. Now you could simply go straight on towards St Day (in which case, continue with the directions at point 10), but it is worth taking the road on the left to visit the attractive Grambler engine house (*). To continue, go back a few yards along the road and take the track on the left (not the path further left to which the public footpath sign points); head towards the church tower at St Day. At the road turn left.

GWENNAP PIT (Colour picture 3)

Gwennap Pit was probably originally formed by the collapse of an old mine working. It is said to have been used for cock-fighting before its association with Methodism. One windy Autumn day in 1762, John Wesley, who had been preaching regularly since 1743 to "innumerable multitudes" among the "unparalleled and inexhaustible mine workings" of Gwennap parish, sought shelter here and preached to a congregation "commodiously placed, row upon row." Over the next 27 years he preached here 17 more times, to congregations which he estimated to range from twenty to twenty-three thousand people - a surprising claim, even allowing for the fact that "they stood far beyond the edge of the pit on all sides." ("I think this is my *ne plus ultra,"* he wrote in September 1781. "I shall scarcely see a larger congregation till we meet in the air.") A nearby mine was re-christened "Cathedral Mine" because Gwennap Pit was "the Cathedral of Methodism". The Pit was converted from its natural form to the present sculpted rows of seats in 1806. A service is still held here annually at the Spring Bank Holiday. The unusual panels at the entrance were created by Guy Sanders between 1986 and 1987 to mark the 250th anniversary of the founding of Methodism. On 13 April 1991 a new visitor centre, linked to the refurbished chapel, was officially opened. The work has been done thanks to £21,000 contributed by Methodists worldwide.

THE GRAMBLER

Grambler (or Grambler & St Aubyn, or East Wheal Sparnon: such name-changes as these affected many Cornish mines, and help make life difficult for amateur industrial archaeologists) was another copper mine which closed in the early 1870s. It re-opened soon after under yet another name, St Aubyn United, and finally ceased production in 1893. The St Aubyns, of course, one of the great landowning families of Cornwall, are associated particularly with Clowance (see *A View from Carn Brea*, Walk 8) and St Michael's Mount. The name "Grambler" derives from *cromlech,* an ancient dolmen or quoit (burial chamber); if there is one nearby, I haven't discovered it.

10 At the Star Inn, on the main road, bear right. You are now at Vogue, whose name comes from the Cornish word for a furnace. Ignore the road forking right (Tolcarne Road), and turn left, along a narrow road called Pink Moors. (An old mine called Wheal Pink was along here, on the left as the road turns right into countryside.)

11 The road leads into woodland. After about half a mile, turn left at the T-junction. This pretty road through the woods eventually turns into a path, and you have a view of Scorrier House (*) on the left.

12 At the main road, turn left. (Please be careful: this is a busy road. Cross to face the oncoming traffic.) After about 300 yards you pass the lodge at the main entrance to Scorrier House. Just after this, and just before a double gate on the right, turn right on to a small path into woodland. (There is a drain grid where it starts.) Come here in May if you can, to enjoy the

SCORRIER HOUSE AND THE POLDICE TRAMWAY

Scorrier House has since 1778 been the home of the Williams family, who (sometimes in partnership with the Harveys of Hayle, the Foxes of Falmouth and others) were a leading force in mining for much of the nineteenth century as well as being actively involved in many related aspects of Cornish industry, such as the iron foundry at Perranarworthal (Walk 10) and the Kennall Vale gunpowder works (Walk 9). Polsue notes in LPH that Scorrier House "contains the most valuable variety of Cornish minerals, that was ever collected by any gentleman in the county." No doubt many of the finest specimens came from the mines they controlled in and near St Day, such as Wheal Unity. The private mineral tramway they built to link Poldice Mine with Portreath on the north coast was Cornwall's first railway, apart from some underground in mines. Work began at Portreath in 1809; the line reached Scorrier House by 1812 and Poldice by 1819. The wagons were horse-drawn, and a carriage designed to carry the directors is currently undergoing restoration at Bristol Museum; John Stengelhofen thinks "it may well be the oldest surviving railway passenger carriage anywhere" (CRH). The line closed in the 1850s, but much of its course can still be traced. It will form an important part of the Mineral Tramways cross-Cornwall route when that is established, and I have included the bulk of it on round walks in PV and *A View from Carn Brea.* For a detailed account of the history of the tramway, see ECMH Vol.2. Scorrier House was largely rebuilt after a disastrous fire in 1908.

bluebells. There are various tracks, and it doesn't matter much which you take so long as you stay in the wooded patch. When you reach a metal fence, go through the gate and then over to the right-hand side of the copse, where the path continues. Later it curves left, then right again. A wooden section near the left side enables you to cross a barbed-wire fence easily; the path now keeps left for a while, and finally bears right and brings you to a wooden fence-stile.

13 Turn left on the lane. Where the lane bears left and goes to a gate, carry straight on along the narrow path which runs by a wall on your right. Cross a stile on the right of a metal gate, and turn left to visit the restored Hawke's Shaft engine house of Killifreth Mine (*). Continue along the track and over a stile by a gate, till you come to the road - another busy one with fast traffic.

14 Turn right and continue for about a quarter of a mile till you reach a crossroads. For a worthwhile short diversion, turn right (signposted Todpool) to have a closer look at three more buildings from the Killifreth complex: the stack on the left, which served an arsenic calciner; the fine stamps-engine house also on the left; and at the end of a short track on the right another pumping-engine house at Old Sump Shaft, which has also been restored. The cylinder of its 50-inch engine was set down into its foundation, or loading, to reduce the overall height of the house, resulting in an odd-looking interior. A single wall is all that now remains of the whim (*) engine house. In common with many other Cornish mine buildings, this was the victim of an army demolition exercise during World War 2. For a

KILLIFRETH MINE

Collins calls Killifreth "an old mine". From 1826 to 1860 it produced mainly copper, and then in 1864 a new company began working it for tin, "with excellent results," according to Collins; but "later," he adds, "the management launched out into expensive schemes of development without previously securing a working capital, with the result that the mine was abandoned in a sort of panic in the year 1896 when practically paying its way." The breakage of the bob of the main pumping engine was partly responsible for the closure. For a time after this the mine was used by the Truro Mining School. In 1911 it re-opened on an ambitious scale, when a Cornish-built 85" pumping engine from a North Wales lead mine was squeezed into the empty engine house on Hawke's shaft; the brick-built upper part of the stack was doubled in height to increase the draught in the boilers. Now that the 150-foot chimney at Tresavean (Walk 13) has gone Killifreth must have a claim to being Cornwall's tallest engine-house stack. Arsenic was produced here in the mine's latter years. Killifreth finally closed in February 1928, although there is still reported to be plenty of tin underground. Some details about the restoration work recently carried out on the Hawke's and Old Sump Shaft engine houses are in PV.

WHIM

This was the winding-gear to raise ore "to grass". (The miners themselves had to climb ladders till the introduction of the "man-engine": see the note on Tresavean, Walk 13. In *A View from Carn Marth* I wrote "the notorious man-engine", and Mr Allen Buckley in a review pointed out the great benefits it brought. In my own defence I would say that as a result of the appalling accident at Levant in 1919, the device has acquired a lurid image, however unjustly.) The early whims were turned by horses, as shown in photographs 71 and 91 in MC, and some of these continued in use into this century; horizontal cylinder engines, or rotative beam-engines like the one preserved by the National Trust at East Pool, were necessary for deeper mines.

drawing based on an old photograph showing three engine houses at Killifreth, see page 11. Now return to the crossroads and go straight on, following the sign to Wheal Busy. The arsenic calciner on the right is intact in many details and repays close inspection. (For information about arsenic production, see the first note on Walk 3.) From there continue to the imposing remains of Great Wheal Busy (*). After inspecting them take the track on the right of the hill covered with mine-spoil, so that at first you are walking towards the main road. Soon the track curves left towards Chacewater (*). Continue for a good half mile, with Chacewater church across the valley on your right. The track becomes an attractive lane down into the village. Bear left at the T-junction, and continue till you come to the road. Turn right, and you emerge on the main street near the King's Head and the car park.

GREAT WHEAL BUSY (Colour pictures 4 and 5)

Great Wheal Busy, formerly called Chacewater Mine, dates back at least to the start of the 18th century. During the 1770s, two steam engines of historical importance were erected here: a large Smeaton atmospheric engine and the first Watt engine to be used at a Cornish mine. Another large Watt engine was erected in 1811. "It had a boilerhouse and stepped stack on each side," Kenneth Brown tells me: "its appetite for coal must have been enormous!" Busy's greatest period was as a copper mine from about 1815 to 1870; after that its main output was arsenic. The boilerhouse attached to the fine engine-house is in good order and still in use as a workshop. The nearby old building was the smithy and fitting shop; notice the impressive cast-iron lintels, made at Perran Foundry (Walk 10) in 1872 when a major expansion of the mine took place. That particular working lasted only a year. In MC there is an

The smithy at Great Wheal Busy

interesting sequence of photographs taken around the time when the mine was re-opened in 1907. They show, among other things, the building of the arsenic-works stack which still stands at the end of the "lambreth" flue; the erection of an 85" beam engine, the third engine to occupy the old engine house; and the festivities in Chacewater which greeted the news that the old mine was having a new lease of life. To help the celebrations along, a bullock for roasting was presented by Viscount Falmouth, then as now the owner of most of this area. Early in 1989 Lord Falmouth's name appeared in the headlines when a £100 million scheme called "Wheal Busy for Cornwall" was published, proposing the building of 1,750 houses, plus industrial estates, a "Cornish food park", a hotel, a leisure park and what was described as a "European airport". Lord Falmouth's agent expressed the view that few were likely to object to the plans, but in fact the Wheal Busy Area Residents'

Association conducted a spirited campaign against them which attracted much support. Carrick District and Cornwall County Councils commissioned a study of the airport project which in March 1990 rejected the idea on the grounds that there was neither the need nor the space for such an airport. John Shields, a member of the Residents' Association, believes that while the current recession lasts little more is likely to happen, but the scheme still exists in modified form, with proposals for fewer houses, smaller industrial units and a golf course instead of the airport.

CHACEWATER

"Chacewater" means "hunting-ground by the water" and may refer to the hunting-ground of the early kings of Cornwall, mentioned in the Tristan legend: see the note on Goodern Manor, Walk 1. Like St Day, it became very populous with the growth of the mining industries and has many interesting Georgian and Victorian houses. The Hornblower family, celebrated for their pioneering work on Cornish beam engines, lived in or near Chacewater from about 1760. Whether Joseph Hornblower lived in this district is uncertain, but his son Jonathan and his wife Ann lived at Salem, just south of Wheal Busy, and after the birth of their third child moved to Whitehall, a little closer to Scorrier. The first three children were Jabez, Jethro and Joanna; while at Whitehall Ann presented her husband with Jesse, Jemima (who apparently died young), Jonathan, Joseph, another Jemima, Julia, Jecholia, Jedida, Jerusha and Josiah. Chacewater church, built in 1827 (not 1837, as I previously wrote), was once famous for its ugliness, but was given an extensive face-lift in 1892. At that time its seating capacity was cut from about 1,500 to 500, an interesting reflection on the decline of the mines.

Based on a photograph taken about 1897, this sketch gives some idea of the size of the bobs used in beam engines. This one weighed 40 tons and was made at the Perran Foundry about 1869 for a lead mine in Wales.

WALK 3

BISSOE, CARHARRACK AND GWENNAP

About seven and a half miles

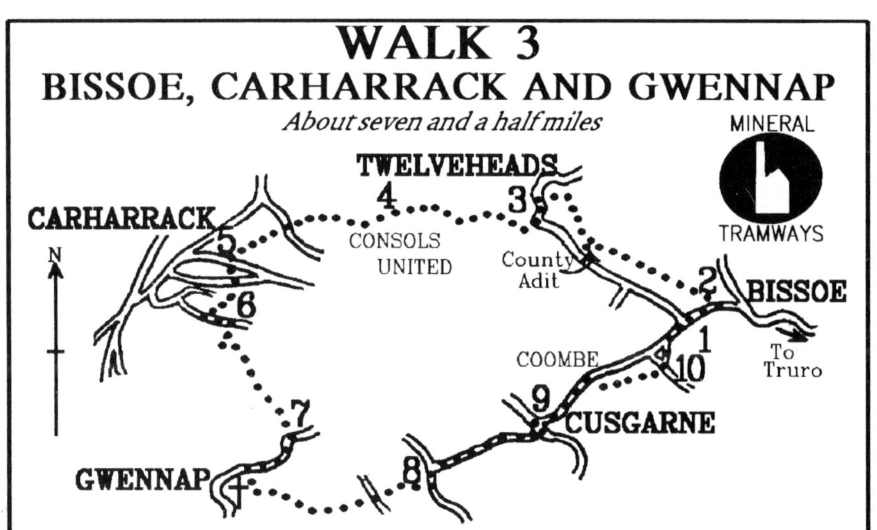

As well as being enormously rich in terms of industrial archaeology, this walk features almost the starkest contrast imaginable within such a confined area: between the bleak industrial desert left by the huge United and Consols copper mines, and the quiet woods, rolling farmland, streams, watermills and pretty rural villages which make up the second half of the route. There is much less road walking than in Walk 2, and you will need good waterproof footwear for the footpath from Gwennap. It is quite a long walk and cannot easily be shortened, but there is a pub conveniently placed at Carharrack; Bissoe and Carharrack also have shops. A short diversion would bring you to the shop and pub at Frogpool: see point 8 in the directions.

To drive to Bissoe from Truro, take the A39 south towards Falmouth. After about five miles you reach the turning to Devoran on the left; a few hundred yards later, take the turning on the right signposted Bissoe. At the crossroads, continue ahead along the valley and under the viaduct carrying the Falmouth branch line (notice the pillars of Brunel's original structure beside it). Drive through Bissoe. Soon after passing the entrance to Cornish Concrete Products (on the left), you could probably park on the large area of waste ground on the right just before the bridge - but see the comments below on "hot rocks" drilling; otherwise, you will need to look for roadside parking, but suitable places for that are not easy to find here, I'm afraid. One possibility would be beside Hick's Mill Chapel (near point 10 on the map), but please remember that this space is needed by members of the congregation during services.

1 Directions start on the opposite side of the river from the extensive former corn mill called Point Mills, at the area of waste ground just mentioned. Early in 1989, plans were announced for drilling over four and a half miles ("the deepest hole ever bored in Britain", it was said) into the earth's crust on this site, as part of a "hot rocks project", similar to but unconnected with the one at Rosemanowes (Walk 8). Mention was made of using a "robotised drilling rig" to reach granite at a temperature of 230° C. Despite vigorous

THE CARNON VALLEY

The Carnon, or Bissoe, Valley has, over thousands or perhaps millions of years, collected vast quantities of alluvial tin, washed down from the granite hills inland. According to HPG, remains of ancient forests are "buried beneath deposits exceeding fifty feet in thickness that overlie the stream tin." Long before anyone thought of mining underground, tin was obtained here by "streaming" - basically, shovelling away the mud, collecting the gravel beneath and extracting the metal from that. The resulting wasteland is now gradually being landscaped and re-planted, but streaming was, at least till 1989, still being carried out on a large scale beside the embankment carrying the A39. Further details connected with this are given in the notes on Walk 11. The availability of water-power, the closeness of the Gwennap mines, and the presence of other minerals such as ochre washed from the mine workings, have led to the development of many other industries in the valley. See the note on Bissoe Bridge in Walk 1.

local protest, planning permission was granted, but little more seems to have been heard of the project by the spring of 1991. Return to the road and turn left (that is, away from Point Mills).

2 Opposite the entrance to Cornish Concrete Products turn left again. This track, taking you up the Carnon Valley (*), is part of the course of the Redruth and Chasewater Railway (*), and if you are sharp-eyed you will occasionally see evidence of this in the form of granite "setts" or sleeper-blocks, originally laid in rows about four feet apart. Cast-iron "chairs" were bolted to them, and these held the wrought-iron rails. The old concrete building on the left (unless it disappears down the shaft!) was a hardcore plant. The large industrial building with winding-gear on the hill ahead is Mount Wellington Mine (*). The prominent engine house to the right of it on Shear's engine shaft dates from the 1820s and is therefore one of the oldest in Cornwall. Kenneth Brown has pointed out that its design is almost identical to that of Taylor's 85" on Consols (1826-7). It housed a 70" pumping engine, later re-cylindered to 65". The separate stack beside it is probably equally old. To the left of that is the newer whim-engine house, so shrouded in ivy that in summer it looks like a tree. All these belonged to the Cusvey section of Consolidated Mines. Go on along the track above the Carnon River, whose banks are stained by ochre, a waste product from the mines which was used by at least one paint-works nearby. Soon you pass the tall "burrows" or waste tips of Nangiles Mine on the right, and may just be able to glimpse what remains of an engine house perched above them. For a note on Nangiles, see Walk 4. Next you will see the village of Twelveheads nestling in its valley on the right, and in a while the walk will take you along the path to it; but first follow the main track a bit further as it curves left

A granite sett complete with cast-iron "chair" (Devoran)

THE REDRUTH AND CHASEWATER RAILWAY

The Redruth and Chasewater was Cornwall's first true railway, in the sense of employing wagons with flanged wheels, unlike the Poldice Tramway (see Walk 2). When mines in the southern part of Gwennap parish, such as Consols, began to be very productive, in the early 1820s, an efficient link with a south coast port became increasingly necessary, for the export of copper ore to South Wales for smelting (Cornwall having no coal deposits), and the import of coal. (During one year in the 1830s, Consols and United Mines alone consumed 15,000 tons of coal.) The new line was officially opened in January 1826, and by 1827 it extended from Wheal Buller, near Redruth, to Point, a mile beyond Devoran on Restronguet Creek. A branch line through Twelveheads to Chacewater was planned but never built. Horses drew the wagons until steam locomotives were introduced in 1854, except on the section below Devoran and on the branch lines serving the Consols and United complex. At first there were two engines, called Miner and Smelter; a third, Spitfire, was added in 1859, by which time the line was handling 90,000 tons of freight per year. The railway closed in 1915, but most of its course can still be traced. More information is in the notes on Walk 11 and in PV. The history of the railway is traced in detail in RCW. Many people are puzzled by the spelling, "Chasewater". I have heard it said that this was simply a mistake on the part of a company official in London, but there is in fact some evidence that it was the usual spelling at the time the railway was formed.

MOUNT WELLINGTON MINE

An old mine called Wheal Friendship was previously on this site. It was last worked by two brothers called Wellington during the 1930s, and the modern mine is named after them; locally, though, it is usually known as Magpie Mine. Following the rise in world tin prices during the 1960s, several new mining ventures were launched in Cornwall; Wheal Jane was the first, in 1971, and Mount Wellington began full production in 1976. By that year the main shaft was already about a thousand feet deep, and the aim was to treat 600 tonnes of ore per day, using a work-force of about 300. Subsequent events have already been outlined in the note on Wheal Jane, Walk 1.

across the valley on an embankment and over a bridge (both built to carry the mineral railway) to a road. If you walk down on the left where the track meets the road you will be able to take a closer look at the bridge. A little closer to the road, water issues from a culvert, through a metal grid and along a narrow cutting to join the Carnon River a few yards downstream. This is the by-pass recently made in the County Adit (*), one of the more surprising engineering feats of Cornwall's industrial past. Now return to the track above, go back over the bridge and take the path to the left after a few yards, leading up the side-valley, complete with tiny stream, to Twelveheads (*). The concrete structures at the start of this path are part of the County Adit, as reconstructed in recent years. Bear right and join the wider track by the house sign for Hillside and Wheal Widden. Turn left over the

THE COUNTY ADIT

Tin and copper lodes usually "underlie" (dip) steeply, so as mining progresses drainage problems increase. Pumping was expensive, even when adequate machinery was available, so wherever possible drainage tunnels (adits) were dug, and their mouths are dotted all over the mining areas on the sides of hills and cliffs, and in valleys, as here. The County (or Great) Adit, begun in 1748 by John Williams, then manager of Poldice Mine, is unique in draining about sixteen square miles and serving over sixty mines; in theory it is possible to walk underground all the way from Wheal Peevor, the fine group of three engine houses beside the A30, to here. Including the many side branches, there are nearly forty miles of tunnel, the deepest parts of which are over four hundred feet down. Additions and improvements to the system, such as the driving of a second adit to cope with the increased water flow as more mines were added and the original ones were extended, continued till the 1880s. The modern mouth of the adit is at the end of a by-pass section which had to be built when the original channels became blocked by landfalls; before that, the water flowed out further down the valley, roughly opposite Nangiles Mine. The bit that has been opened out into a cutting shows how small a space those who built the Adit had to work in.

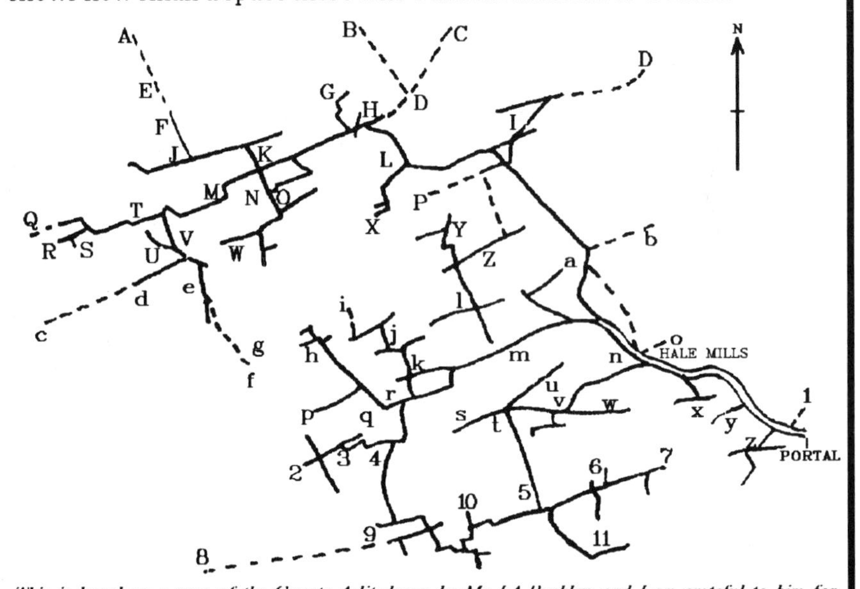

This is based on a map of the County Adit drawn by Mr J.A.Buckley, and I am grateful to him for permission to use it. It is the result of several years' research and is, he tells me, probably still incomplete, but gives some idea of the complexity of the system. Broken lines indicate sections added at a late stage.
The mines shown are: A Mawla & Stencoose; B Briton; C North Busy; D Boscawen; E Barberry; F North Briggan; G East Downs; H Halenbeagle; I Chacewater (Great Wheal Busy); J Briggan; K Hawke; L East Chance; M Messer; N South Hawke; O Chance; P Killifreth; Q Treleigh Consols; R Maria; S Good Success; T Peevor; U Prussia; V Boys; W Treskerby; X Scorrier; Y Union; Z North Unity; a Creegbrawse; b St Michael Penkevil; c Harmony & Treleigh Wood; d Cardrew; e Derrick; f Trefula; g Lilly; h Pink (now we know where Scaffold got their title); i Clinton; j Gorland; k Quick; l Unity; m Poldice; n Killicor; o Henry (no comment); p Roselabby; q Tolcarne; r Jewell; s Carharrack; t West Virgin; u Maid; v Virgin; w Lovelace; x Fortune; y Cusvey; z Friendship; 1 Nangiles; 2 Hope; 3 Spinster; 4 Damsel; 5 Poldory; 6 Ale & Cakes; 7 East Ale & Cakes; 8 Pennance; 9 Ting Tang; 10 Squire; 11 South Ale & Cakes.

TWELVEHEADS

The stamping machines used for crushing ore frequently had twelve heads; there was one such here, operated by a water-wheel. (See page 12 for a picture of a set of stamps with twelve heads, taken from one of the illustrations in the catalogue published by Williams' Perran Foundry in the early 1870s.) Twelveheads was the birthplace of the evangelical preacher, Billy Bray: see Walks 1 and 4. Another Twelveheads man, Nigel Oates, became well known locally for his singing and violin-playing after he had been blinded in an accident in a copper mine.

footbridge.

3 At the road turn left, crossing a second bridge. Where the road bends left, take the track straight ahead. Before long there is a tarmac drive on the left, and on the right opposite this is a sunken, grassy track. This is where the old railway-line continues, and it is a public right of way, but when I was last there brambles and other growth made it impassable. If you continue for about a hundred yards and take the next track on the right, you will find that after a short distance (about 20 yards after a wooden post on the left) there is a steepish path down into the valley on the right, re-joining the railway track just after the overgrown patch. Now follow this - two black pipes (later just one) mark its course clearly. (Recently, however, some of them have been removed. - March 1991.) The pipes were laid to carry "tailings" from Mount Wellington to a reservoir which you will see later. In this area are many old mine-shafts capped with metal "cages" known as Clwyd caps. The old method of capping consisted of boarding over the shaft a few feet down and topping off with rubble and soil - a recipe for trouble when the wood rotted. Clwyd caps are obviously a great improvement on that, but are looked on less favourably now than at first, perhaps partly because they have not always been installed in the way the inventor intended. Soon after the fenced-off shaft on the right the track becomes a leafy path, rather overgrown with gorse. This goes through a cutting and under a bridge: as you pass beneath it, look up to see how it has been constructed from old rails, possibly salvaged from the line, although the bridge was rebuilt a good many years after the line was taken up. Soon afterwards, look right to see the embankment and bridge which were built in 1853-4 to carry a branch line to Wheal Busy via Poldice, Unity Wood and Killifreth mines. (Details of the history of this branch are given in PV.) The line was never completed, but the bridge, with its twin tunnels for stream and track, is worth going down to inspect more closely. A special quarry was created nearby to obtain the masonry for lining the tunnels.

4 The walk continues in the same direction as before, past an old rusty hopper, and up a short slope on to the top of a wall of the tailings dam of Mount Wellington Mine (*). (Colour picture 8. See Walk 1 for a note on tailings dams.) Go up the track on the left and through a gate. All around you now are the spoil-heaps of Consolidated and United Mines (*), one of the most desolate scenes of industrial dereliction in Cornwall - though the reason for that is mainly the way man has treated it during this century: Left to its own devices, nature would probably have clothed it all in gorse and

CONSOLS AND UNITED MINES (Colour picture 8)

Great Consolidated Mines and United Mines were both amalgamations of several smaller mines which had proved very rich in copper during the latter part of the 18th century. They began losing money before the turn of the century, mainly because of competition from Anglesey, and both groups had closed down by 1805, but in 1811 United was restarted, soon coming under the influence of the Williamses of Scorrier, and in 1819 the Norwich-born businessman John Taylor re-opened Consols. The latter venture was a huge and almost immediate success: from 1823 to 1840 Consols' annual output of copper oustripped all its rivals, including Dolcoath. In 1824 Taylor took over United. When the time came for his lease of Consols to be renewed, in 1839, his Cornish competitors ensured that his application was refused, and his response was to "pick the eyes out" of the mine, that is, he stripped it of all available ore including underground stockpiles. From that year onwards, Consols' output dropped steadily, and eventually, in 1857, it was taken over by United; Clifford Amalgamated Mines, as the company then named itself, closed in 1869. For much of the preceding fifty-or-so years, Consols/Clifford was the world's biggest copper mine, with over eighty miles of underground workings and eighteen engine-houses; nearly a million tons of copper, plus some tin and other metals, were brought up. Surprisingly little now remains on the surface, although the ruined engine-house just below the clock tower is of special interest as one of the oldest in Cornwall. The great burrows, still strangely impressive, however ugly, have been depleted, much of the waste material having been removed for road-making; some parts have been landscaped and replanted, another used for an industrial estate. One of the tips, called Davey's Burrow, "was said to have been as high as Truro Cathedral when Consols was stopped," according to RCR. "In this scene of desolation," Barton writes, "it is not easy to reconstruct it in the mind's eye as it was in its heyday in the 1830's; noisy with steam whims on the drawing shafts, the roar of ore-crushers, and the quieter motion of the big pumping-engines, the whole scene busy with miners and surface workers moving to and fro across the complex layouts of shafts, headgears, pulley stands, ore storage and dressing floors, cobbing and bucking houses, miner's dries, barracks and other sheds, all laced by leats and launders, tram-road branches and cart-tracks." (Cobbing and bucking were methods of breaking up lumps of ore to separate it from waste.) An equally vivid description of Consols was written by the novelist William Beckford following his visit in 1787; I have quoted part of it in PV (page 49), and the rest is in HPG.

heather. Turn right and walk by the fence on your right; ignore the right fork down into the valley, and continue under the old engine-houses. After the line of four rusty posts across the track, turn up on your left. As you approach a fenced-off shaft on the right, bear left up a stony ramp, and walk on past the engine-house to the base of the Consols clock-tower. You can go inside this via a granite archway. The clock was used in St Day for many years after Consols closed, and the "movement" is now being restored. From here return to the lower track by the same route, turning left between the three rusty posts. Go down the lower, right-hand track, past an old electricity sub-station, then between iron gate-posts and along a lane - the old railway track again - forking left to reach a road at the edge of Crofthandy. Cross the road and continue on the track opposite or a few yards to your left, between wire fences. This is still the railway track. A little further on, barbed wire had been draped across the path when I last was there, but it was easy to duck under. Continue beside the hedge on the right. The large ruined building ahead was the railway's Great Yard, built about 1851 to house an office and eight storage bays for coal and other items, plus probably stables for the horses used on the extensive system serving United and Consols which branched off the main line here. You can walk through the Great Yard. The path then continues by the hedge on the left, past a group of pines, and reaches the road via a metal farm gate.

5 Carharrack (*) is well worth exploring, especially to see relics of the railway - and you may well by now be ready for one of the excellent pasties

CARHARRACK

The name seems to mean "fort of the high place", perhaps a hint that Carn Marth was, as seems very likely, once fortified. The whole area was probably quite thickly wooded (compare the note on Lanner, Walk 13). According to HPG, there were just twelve cottages at Carharrack in 1770, but copper mining and the coming of the railway soon changed that. Polsue describes it as "a populous and respectable village" (LPH). (In recent years, much interesting material about the history of Carharrack has been gathered by local historians, notably Eric Rabjohns and Barrie May; their exhibition was on display at the Methodist Church for the second time in 1990, and if it is given further airings I'd strongly recommend a visit.) The Redruth and Chasewater Railway ran through the centre of the village. To see the clearest evidence of the railway's course, walk on past Mills's Hall (named after William John Mills, a businessman from St Day who devoted much of his wealth to local causes) and the Seven Stars and turn right at the main road, which at this point is called Railway Terrace. After about a hundred yards, just to the right of a 30 mph sign on a lamp-post, there are parallel old stone walls. This was the line, and if you turn round you will see how it crossed the road and passed in front of a terrace of houses and behind the shops. You could now walk back past the shops and take the first right turning (crossing the course of the line). Turn left in front of the chapel (note its date: just when copper mining was moving into top gear) and along the path. There is an old iron lamp-standard beside the drive which follows the railway track. Cross Wheal Damsel Road. Notice how sleeper blocks have been incorporated in the garden wall of the corner house; this was once a pub, The Steam Engine, and the old photograph my drawing is based on shows Spitfire and her crew proudly posing in front of it. Walk up the road ahead, and soon on your left you will see a small cutting crossed by an original footbridge, recently restored by Carharrack Parish Council. To continue the walk, return past the Seven Stars and take the first main right turning, Sparry Lane. Follow this as it turns right, and continue out of the village. Now follow the directions from point 6.

Spitfire in front of the Steam Engine pub, Carharrack

served up at the Seven Stars. To walk into Carharrack, turn right at the road and keep left at the crossroads; directions for looking round the village and re-joining the walk route are included in the Carharrack note. To continue the walk without going into Carharrack, turn left at the road and after a few yards take the track on the right. Cross the next road and continue on the track ahead, which soon becomes a footpath. Turn left when you reach another road.

6 Fork right where marked Little Sparry Farm. Where the high wire-mesh fence stops, turn left, and walk with the fence left and the wood right. Keep to the main track, which manages to be pretty despite the vast tip to the left.

7 After about half a mile you reach a road. Turn right, and follow the road as it bends left towards Gwennap (*). On the edge of the village cross the bridge on the left, walking beside the churchyard. At the corner, turn right to look at the church and village; but the main walk-route takes you through the kissing-gate on the left at the corner. Now go across the upper part of the field and cross a stile on the right of a gate. Keep by the hedge on the right: the next stile is at the right-hand corner of the field. Next head just left of the nearest pylon, where a stile crosses the wall; then cross the following field to a stile on the right of gates. After this, keep by the fence on your left, go through the narrow gap and cross the next stile. Cross the road to a low granite style beside a footpath sign to Cusgarne. The path now continues in a fairly straight line over three more stiles to another road.

GWENNAP

Gwennap village, surrounded by woodland, seems to be in another world from the industrial dereliction on its doorstep. The church, with its separate tower (compare Feock, on Walk 11), dates from the 15th century; like nearly every old Cornish church, it was much restored in Victorian times. The large graveyard gives some indication of the enormous growth in population in Gwennap parish that was caused by the copper-mining boom, and many of the headstones are worth study from that point of view. The village, the churchyard and the nearby mines were used imaginatively by David Wiseman as the setting for his novel for young people, *The Fate of Jeremy Visick.*

8 Turn left, and take the next turning on the right, which comes just after a layby. This pretty little road runs beside a stream, past an old water-mill, and after about half a mile brings you into the attractive village of Cusgarne ("crane wood" or possibly "heron wood"), with its old mill building and two streams. *(If at this point you need refreshments, turn right at the T-junction in Cusgarne and follow the road past the school and into Frogpool, where you will find a general store and a pub, the Cornish Arms, well known for good food. This would add a distance of about half a mile each way.)* One of the houses in Cusgarne was the home for nearly twenty years (1781-1800) of James Watt, who in partnership with Matthew Boulton dominated the supply of steam engines to Cornish mines during that period. He was in bad health when he first came to Cusgarne, but soon afterwards his wife wrote, "James's spirits are surprising since his arrival. This is a delightful place..." The elm trees that surrounded her walled garden are gone now, but Cusgarne is delightful still. At the T-junction in the village, turn left.

9 Turn right (signposted to Bissoe), and at the next small group of houses (Coombe) right again, crossing the stream; then go left by a footpath sign, over a leat serving Hick's Mill, and along the footpath beside the stream. Later you cross the leat again. After Hick's Mill Church, notice the mill on your left, now being restored. One of the two old waterwheels is still in place and parts of the other one lie nearby. On the skyline to the left is Wheal Jane.

10 Turn left at the road, then bear right to Point Mills, now looking much more cared-for than it did when I researched the original *Carn Marth.* Almost opposite Point Mills is a track leading to what was till 9th December 1990 a tall, tapering chimney, once part of the Bissoe Arsenic Works (*). During a storm that night the stack was almost completely destroyed by lightning. (Colour pictures 9 and 10.) It was left in a dangerous state, and the local authority proposed to demolish what remained, but in response to local protests it was given a stay of execution, and there is some hope that funds may become available (perhaps via the Poldice Valley Trust) for some reconstruction. Kenneth Brown believes it to be the only square stack surviving in West Cornwall. Continue over the bridge and back to your car. Notice as you walk this part the remains of various leats that once served several waterwheels lower down the valley.

THE CORNWALL ARSENIC COMPANY WORKS AT BISSOE

Arsenic was once regarded merely as a troublesome by-product of tin-mining. During the 19th century, its value in various industrial processes began to be understood (later it also became widely used in herbicides and pesticides), and during times of financial crisis in the tin and copper trade mine-owners began extracting it from waste material. The ore was roasted, and the resulting gases were funnelled through long "lambreth" (= labyrinth) flues ending with a tall chimney to create a strong draught, leaving on the walls an arsenic deposit which then had to be scraped off. An interesting photograph showing a workman shovelling arsenic dust out of flues, his nose plugged with cotton-wool, is printed in IAC. The story of Cornish arsenic production is fascinatingly told by D.B.Barton in ECMH, Vol.2, and I have included a section about it in PV. Bissoe plays a leading part in that story: there were three important works here, two of which survived well into this century. Around the waste heaps here you may - especially in hot weather - be able to detect the characteristic smell, rather like garlic. Much of the soil downstream of the works is one-part-in-200 arsenic, reputedly the highest concentration anywhere in the world. Few if any plants can survive in that, but the Cornwall Trust for Nature Conservation is making valiant efforts to restore the land; in some areas hundreds of tons of mud dredged from the Fal estuary are being used to provide a cap at least six inches deep.

If you drive back by the same route as described at the start, you will be more-or-less following the course of the old railway. On the right just past the crossroads is the old stack of a vitriol works. At the A39, just before you make the left turning for Truro notice the level-crossing gate a little to the right on the opposite side - a modern copy of the original one.

WALK 4
A SHORT WALK AROUND TWELVEHEADS AND NANGILES

About a mile

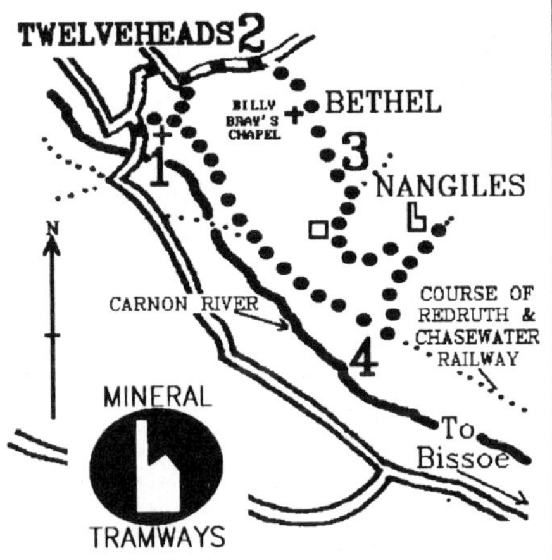

This is what in some other books I have called a "Sunday Afternoon Special". A section of it repeats bits of Walks 2 and 3, but I want to include it, partly for its historical interest and partly for the good view it provides over typical Cornish mining scenery. The walk involves climbing and descending quite a steep hill, and the tracks are liable to be muddy in places.

The directions start and end at Twelveheads village, which is almost literally in the shadow of Mount Wellington mine, about a mile north-west of Bissoe. To drive there from Truro, follow the directions at the start of Walk 3. After crossing the bridge at Point Mills, take the first right turning, opposite a filling station. Continue up the valley road, ignoring the left turning, and this brings you into Twelveheads. There is usually space to park in front of the Methodist Church at the centre of the village.

1 Take the path on the left side of the chapel, and after crossing the footbridge bear left up a track. It's easy to see why this pretty and sheltered valley setting attracted settlers, and also why the availability of so much running water brought not only corn mills but the Cornish Stamps machines whose racket must once have made life almost unbearable. To that might have been added the noise of railway engines, but the Chacewater branch of the mineral railway was never in fact built. At the road turn right and continue uphill for about a quarter of a mile. Among some farm buildings on the left, just before a farmhouse, is a very tumbledown cottage which I shall mention again soon.

2 Take the first turning on the right, immediately beyond the farmhouse, a track leading towards quite a large chapel. When you reach it you will see that it bears the inscription, "Bethel Methodist Chapel 1842"; adjoining it is the "Old Schoolhouse", and it is that rather than the main building which is what survives of the first chapel built by Billy Bray (*). From here there is a

BILLY BRAY AND HIS CHAPELS

Twelveheads' most famous son, Billy Bray (1794-1868), a "drunken and lascivious miner" (his own words) as a young man, became an inspiring evangelistic preacher of the Bible Christian Methodist Church. "Had he lived 1,000 years previously," wrote Charles Henderson in CCG, Billy Bray "would have a church and holy well called after him." One day my wife and I visited Twelveheads purposely to try to find his birthplace, half-expecting to see a commemorative plaque on a tiny cottage, but with

no success. When we came to Bethel we were shown around by Alec Wiles, who uses the old chapel building as a studio for his paintings and sculptures, and he told us that Billy was born in the tumbledown cottage I have referred to. Billy's own account of the building of his first chapel is given in BBKS: "The Lord put it in my mind to build a chapel. My mother had a small place; and by one of her little fields there was a small piece of common. The Lord opened my mother's heart to give a spot on that piece of common to build on. .... I began work as the dear Lord told me, and to take away the hedge of my mother's field, and to dig out the foundation of a chapel ... which was to be called Bethel." He goes on to tell of the opposition which came, not only from "the wicked" but even from some of his own sect; and of his struggles to raise enough funds to carry on. "When my little maid (daughter) was taken ill, Satan tempted me that it would take seven pounds to cover the chapel, and I had but two pounds, and our little one would die, and it would take one pound to bury her, and then I should have but one pound left." But he defied the devil, completed the work, and his daughter went on to bear ten children of her own. He tells how the original little chapel became a schoolhouse when a larger one was built beside it: "No wonder that the devil was so against me while I was building the old Bethel, and put his servants to hinder me, for I have seen at one time fifty down asking for mercy, and mercy they had." Later he built two other chapels, at Kerley Downs west of Baldhu Church, and "Great Deliverance", the largest of the three, at Carharrack. The only one still in use for worship is the so-called "Three Eyes" chapel at Kerley Downs; for some information about that and Billy's grave, see the note on Baldhu in Walk 1.

rather fine view across the valley, with Mount Wellington, Cusvey Mine, the Consols clock tower and St Day Church all on the skyline.

3 Continue along the track, and after about a quarter of a mile take the downhill track on the right, heading towards the Mount Wellington buildings. Soon this brings you to what looks like a miniature triumphal arch perched high above the valley: in fact, a bob wall, all that remains of a fine engine house that was a well-known landmark till this mine, Nangiles (*), was reworked during the 1960s. (The bob wall was the one most strongly built, because it had to bear the weight of the huge "bob" or beam of the engine. In this case the engine was an 80-inch one used for pumping.) Below it are huge waste-tips, and all around, half-hidden by the undergrowth, are many shafts and other excavations. Go on down the track as it curves to the left, and at the T-junction turn left to see the other surface relic of Nangiles - an engine house so thickly shrouded in ivy as to be easily missed, even though it is quite close to the track (on the left). It contained a Cornish-built 36-inch engine which was purchased secondhand in 1871 from an unsuccessful gold mining project in North Wales, along with 84 heads of stamps, all of which had lain unused since 1864! Return the same way, continuing down the main track to the valley floor.

4 Turn right. You are now on the trackbed of the Redruth and Chasewater Railway; there is a note about this in Walk 3, and the rest of this walk, back to Twelveheads, is as described in the latter part of section 2 of Walk 3.

NANGILES MINE (Colour picture 11)

Nangiles, described by W.H.Collins as "a very ancient mine" (OWEMR), produced over 3,000 tons of copper, plus smaller amounts of tin, iron, zinc, arsenic and ochre, between 1845 and 1906. The water in this mine is said to have contained so much vitriol (sulphuric acid) that it would "rot a pair of boots off a man's feet in one day". As a result it was necessary to line the pumps with wood and brass or bronze, and the cost of this ruined the company. A unique feature at Nangiles is a railway with wooden lines seventy feet underground, and again it is thought that wood was chosen because of the acid; this seems to be confirmed by the discovery of a boot with wooden "nails" in one of the workings. (JTS No. 5, 1977.) In 1905 Nangiles became part of Falmouth Consolidated Mines, and in recent years it has been worked along with Mount Wellington and Wheal Jane. Kenneth Brown tells me that "lovely specimens of arsenopyrite may be picked up at Nangiles - a dump on your right as you turn on to the railway is the best place, but it is fenced off."

The Nangiles pumping engine house as it was

WALK 5

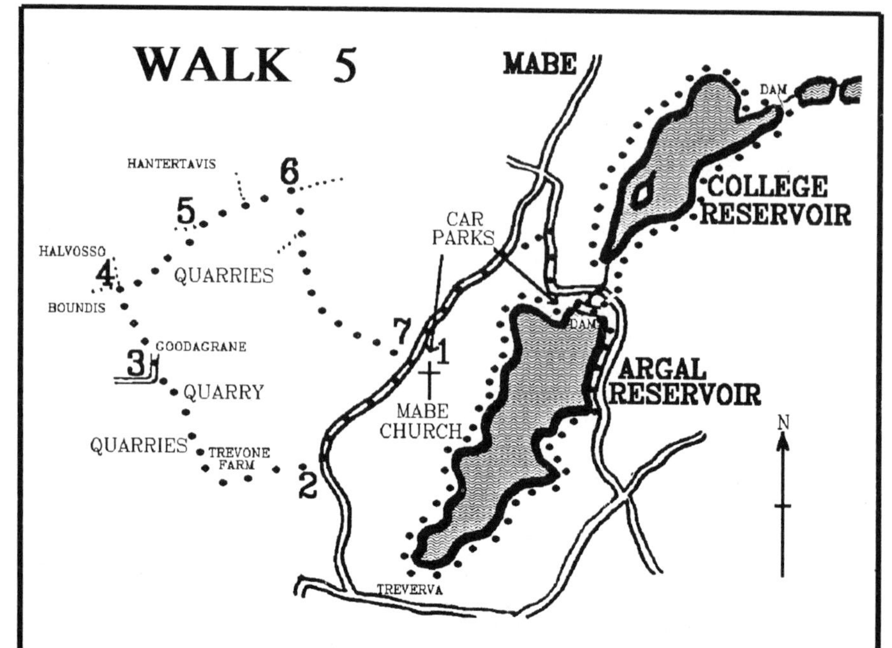

AMID GRANITE QUARRIES AND MAN-MADE LAKES: WALKS FROM MABE CHURCH AND AROUND ARGAL AND COLLEGE RESERVOIRS

One walk of nearly seven miles, or three walks ranging from under two to nearly three miles.

From about 1750 until World War II, quarrying rivalled mining in importance in mid-Cornwall; indeed, there are probably just as many abandoned quarries in the area covered by this book as abandoned mines. (There were over 100 granite quarries within easy reach of the stoneyards and quays of Penryn, according to Q&Q, and presumably that figure ignores the small workings one so frequently sees.) Cornish copper mining is dead and Cornish tin mining seems to be drawing its last few fleeting breaths, but Cornish stone-quarrying lives on, and not only to satisfy the need for hard-core for road building. The silvery-grey granite found around Penryn, Constantine and the parishes between is particularly famous, and a large quarry that is still exploiting it (at Longdowns, on the A394) is visible in the distance on the walk based on Mabe Church, which passes through or close to several abandoned quarries, large and small. (Walk 6 includes a close look at a working quarry.) It is also a very pleasant country walk in its own right (including good views and an ancient and beautiful church), and even better if you have the time to add to it a walk around one or both of the reservoirs. These are smaller and older than Stithians (Walks 7 and 8), and less noted for birdwatching, but scenically more attractive, being set among gently rolling hills, with much more woodland than at Stithians. College and Argal reservoirs have been developed as a valuable leisure amenity by South West Water, and the paths around both are well maintained, with signposts, board-walks, and so on, where needed; even so, you would be wise to wear waterproof shoes or boots. Dog-owners are catered for (a "Dogs' Toilet" is provided, and a separate car park for dog-owners' vehicles), but please note that dogs should be kept on leads on the paths round both reservoirs, in order to protect grazing sheep. The quarries walk was distinctly muddy in places when we did it, has a few quite awkward stiles, and may possibly get rather overgrown at times, but only the faint-hearted will be deterred by all that! It's really quite an easy walk, and I mean that most sincerely. The nearest shops and pub are in Mabe. If you would like to look inside the church, the key can be obtained by prior arrangement from the Rev. C. Firth at the vicarage, which is close to the New Inn; ring 0326-73201.

If you want to do the quarries walk, with or without adding one or both reservoirs, the best place to park would be Mabe Church, on the west side of Argal Reservoir; but for the reservoir walks only, use the visitors' car parks at the northern end of Argal. To drive there from Truro, take the Falmouth road (A39). At Treluswell roundabout (the first roundabout after the Norway Inn), continue ahead on the Helston road (A394) as far as the next (double) roundabout, where you take the third turning off, the minor road into Mabe village, signposted to the Argal and College Water Park. Go straight on at the crossroads in Mabe (past the New Inn, the nearest pub to the walk routes), then take the second right turning for Mabe Church (a minor road going straight on where the main road bears left), or continue on the main road for the Water Park, which is signposted on the right.

The directions begin with the quarries walk, starting at Mabe Church (*). Directions are hardly necessary for the walks round the reservoirs, but for some comments on these see the end of point 7.

1 From the church car park, continue south-west along the road (i.e., past the church).

2 After about a quarter of a mile turn right beside the notice, Trevone Farm, where there is a signed footpath. This begins as a concreted drive, with an attractive valley view to the left and large piles of cut granite at disused quarries (*) both on the right and ahead. Soon you pass a nicely restored large house on the right: granite, naturally, and with hefty granite boulders lining its entrance drive. Not far beyond that is a small group of farm buildings converted into dwellings which make imaginative use of original features such as an opening on the upper floor, presumably where there was once a platform for the hoisting and lowering of grain sacks or other goods. Go through a metal gate and along a rather muddy lane towards the quarries. The lane curves right, and then you go through a metal farm gate and proceed along the most obvious path, which is level and runs on the right

MABE CHURCH (Colour picture 12)

The name "Mabe" is hard to explain, but may derive from a personal name, perhaps that of a saint, although the church is dedicated to St Laudus (otherwise Laud, Lo or Loe), a Breton bishop of the 6th century. The building - granite, of course - is pretty in itself, with a fine pinnacled tower, and the more attractive, it seems to me, because of its isolation and the setting provided by the lake. It dates from the 15th century, but all except the tower and porch was rebuilt after being struck by lightning in February 1866. It has always been locked when I have attempted to enter, so I can do no more that accept Arthur Mee's list of interesting details (in KEC), including "a richly carved 18th century chest, an elaborate old armchair, and an Elizabethan chalice" as well as a fine 16th-century engraved silver-plate cup, though the last two are presumably not normally on view. In the churchyard are a longstone probably dating from the Bronze Age and a Celtic cross; the former is close to the tower and south porch.

GRANITE QUARRYING IN MID-CORNWALL
(Colour pictures 15, 16, 25 and 26)
See also the note on Carnsew Quarry in Walk 6, and pages 138-9.

In the introduction to this walk I have made a few comments on the importance of this industry. For fuller detail I would recommend two small books, namely Q&Q, which includes interesting photographs and is particularly good on the methods used to split and polish the stone; and ASI No.4 (1986). The latter contains a fascinating article by Joyce and Basil Green focusing on Stithians parish but also throwing light on quarrying in Constantine, Mabe, Penryn and other neighbouring parishes. They trace the development of the industry following John Smeaton's use of granite from Constantine in the Eddystone Lighthouse (1759); the 19th-century boom period, when Cornish granite was used for Waterloo, Southwark and London Bridges, and when John Freeman opened 60 quarries in the Penryn area alone; the great decline in our own century, especially since the 1960s; and recent hopeful predictions that "granite is making a comeback". There is an important link between this topic and Walk 9, not only because there is a granite quarry at Kennall Vale, but because gunpowder was so important in granite quarrying. Mr Anthony Cartwright has sent me the following comments: "Gunpowder was preferred to other, more powerful forms of explosive, because it was relatively "gentle" (if one can apply such a term to an explosive!). When extracting dimension stone (i.e. large blocks destined to be shaped for buildings) what was needed was a charge which would ease the block forward from the working face, its shape being determined by the natural joints found in granite. It's interesting to note that in granite (and other) quarries where stone is being extracted as road-metal, more powerful explosives are used, since the object is to shatter the rock into relatively small pieces, thus reducing the amount of subsequent smashing and crushing which must be done."

side of a line of gorse bushes to another metal gate. We were intrigued and a little puzzled to see that the impressive pile of quarried granite on the far side of the valley has a stone building at the right-hand end, similar to a ruined mine engine house, and we weren't sure if we could see the remains of a waterwheel on the side of it. Mrs Joyce Green of the Stithians Local History Group tells me there were in fact two waterwheels in this area that were used to pump the water out of the quarry-pits. The path now runs among deserted and dilapidated corrugated-iron sheds surrounded by cut granite blocks with very clear drill-holes showing how they were split from the parent rock, together with a few shaped and polished pieces, perhaps gravestones, sad relics of a thriving business apparently cut off in its prime, and now inevitably a Mecca for fly-tippers. Soon you reach the flooded quarry itself. The contrasting shapes and textures carved into the clifflike walls by the quarrymen, the natural fissures and the various colour-patterns formed by minerals deposited by trickling water, all reflected in the still, dark pool, together create a strange beauty which is somehow enhanced by the echoing sound of constant dripping from an unseen source. If all that sounds like some "romantick" 18th-century grotto, I'll return to earth by pointing out the relics of the workmen's way of life, such as the ruined shelter, complete with the remains of a fireplace or oven, and the flimsy-looking metal stake projecting from the right-hand wall of the quarry and supporting a rotting plank which presumably once provided access to the rock-face for drilling purposes. Did it look less dangerous when there was no water below? Beyond the quarry, the path crosses a stream, goes uphill and reaches a lane.

3 Turn right on that, through the wooden gate beside the cottage at Goodagrane (probably meaning "streams in the bracken"), and then left (not through the metal gate ahead), over a high but well-maintained stile in the wall, and along a grassy lane. At the end of that, go through the right-hand gate, walk a little way with the hedge on your left, then cross the stile in the corner and continue with the hedge on the right. Ahead now on the skyline is a modern working quarry at Longdowns. (Hawes and Kessel Downs Quarries there are still active.) After the next stile we encountered quite deep mud. Continue ahead and cross a further stile, bringing you to a sunken lane, also rather muddy. (At this point you are close to Halvosso ["rough pasture fields"]; Mrs Green told me about a couple living there 50 years ago who used to go to the pictures in Falmouth on Saturday nights and then walk home, coming up Trescobeas Road and walking across country where the reservoir is now and through the nearby quarries.)

4 Turn right. Ignore the very wide track on the right soon after; go through the gateway ahead (even muddier, I fear!) and then down the full length of the field towards more quarries, heading for the left-hand corner, where the stile is obviously designed for exceptionally tall people. Now go to the right, through a marshy patch, over a small footbridge and a pretty stile, and

then turn left along a path which was clear and perfectly walkable despite some low overhanging branches, but looked as if it could easily get rather overgrown and boggy.

5 The path joins a wider track near some modern stables at Carnebo Farm; go left there. Keep to the track as it curves right, uphill, with quarries on both sides. The track going left from it after a few hundred yards leads to Hantertavis, an intriguing name which may mean "half a tongue", referring apparently to a large rock with a hollow in it.

6 Don't go that way, but take the next track on the right, beside a sign announcing the DGW Sand Co., and then almost immediately fork left. You are now on Spargo Downs; from here in clear weather there is a fine view on the left to Carrick Roads, St Anthony Lighthouse and the sea beyond; closer at hand and almost straight ahead is Mabe Church. Where the track curves right, down towards a quarry, turn left on a narrow footpath through the bracken, fork right and cross the stile on the right. Walk down to the far left corner of the long field, where there is a stile on the right of a muddy gateway. Continue in the same direction with the hedge on your left, over two more stiles and down to the left side of the tree-shrouded former vicarage. Here there are some steps up on to the hedge, and the path continues along the hedge-top beside the vicarage garden for a little way, then down to ground level before reaching the road opposite the church.

7 Now if you want to walk round one reservoir or both, either drive to the car park at Argal or walk along the road back towards Mabe. You pass Lower Spargo ("thorn-hedge") Farm, then cross a stream and go uphill. Beside the entrance to Chynoweth ("new house"), cross the stile on the right. From there go up to another stile at the top-right corner of the field and walk with the hedge on your left to a final stile at the road. Turn right and walk with care, facing the oncoming traffic, which tends to be quite fast along this stretch. After about a quarter of a mile you will reach the entrance to the "Water Park", from which the paths around both College and Argal Reservoirs (*) are signposted. For the College walk you cross first the dam and then the road; the latter requires care because of the fast traffic just mentioned. Much of the perimeter of College reservoir is marshy; board-walks have been created at the wettest sections, but still we were glad of our wellies when we last walked round, after several rainy days. The western side is quite thickly wooded, and in summer you will probably catch only a few glimpses of the water from the path in that area, but the northern and eastern sections are much more open, and the path skirts the water's edge there. The northern end of this reservoir is overlooked by Mabe village, and the newish road linking the Kernick Industrial Estate to Treliever Cross runs close to the water's edge for a few hundred yards. Argal Reservoir is overlooked by the church on the west side and by Treverva village at the southern end. Walkers have good water views almost all the way round, although there are several wooded areas, again on the western side, and among the trees are a few small disused quarries.

COLLEGE AND ARGAL RESERVOIRS
(Colour pictures 12 & 13)

The name "College" refers to the great collegiate church of Glasney, founded by the Bishop of Exeter in 1265, whose buildings ("a church modelled on that of Exeter Cathedral, refectory, and chapter house, with mills," to quote from Dr James Whetter's history of the College, published in 1988) occupied the part of Penryn now identifiable as College Hill, Glasney Field and the lower part of Hillhead. (I can't resist quoting part of John Leland's account, written following his visit in 1538: "One Water Goode [by whom he means Walter Bronescombe, nicknamed "the Good"], Bisshop of Excestre, made yn a More, caullid Glenith, in the Botom of a Park of his at Penrine, a Collegiate Church, cawled S. Thomas, wher be Secular Chanons with a Provost, twelve Prebendaries, and other Ministers. This College is strongly wallid and incastellid, having three strong Towers and Gunnes at the But of the Creke.") College Reservoirs are within the area once forming the Bishop's deer park. The story is often told that the canons from Glasney habitually poached the deer, so Bishop Grandisson in 1330 ordered the doors on that side of the College to be sealed. Below the large reservoir known as "College No.4", which was created in 1906, are at least three much smaller and presumably older man-made pools. Argal Dam was built in 1940 to create a larger reservoir than College No.4, catering for the rapidly growing water-needs of Penryn and Falmouth, and this dam was raised by ten feet in 1961. It takes its name from Argal ("secluded place") Manor, just to the east of the dam.

WORKING QUARRIES AND SPLENDID VIEWS: MABE, GONORMAN DOWNS AND ROSKROW

WALK 6

About four and a half miles. Could be linked to Walk 9, making a total of about ten miles. (See the end of point 5.)

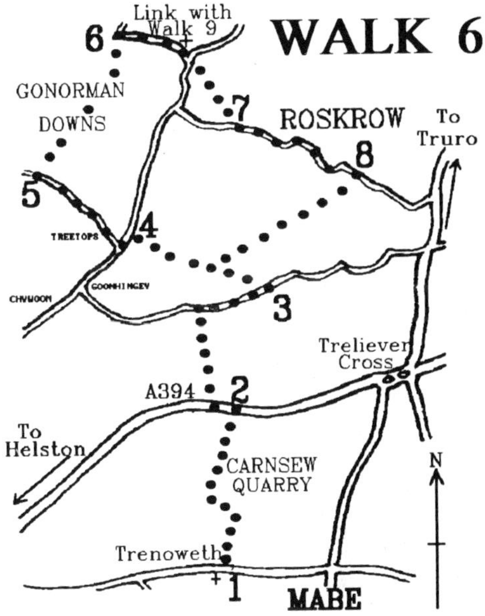

Link with Walk 9
GONORMAN DOWNS
ROSKROW
To Truro
TREETOPS
CHYWOON
GOONHINGEY
Trelieven Cross
A394
To Helston
CARNSEW QUARRY
Trenoweth
MABE
N

PLEASE NOTE: A sign on the north side of the quarry which this walk runs beside warns that blasting takes place between 1530 and 1750 hrs. If you plan to do the walk on a weekday, therefore, you should avoid this period, or else omit that part of the walk. An alternative starting point could be at SW 760353, on the minor road running east from Goonhingey and Chywoon; the road is narrow, but the verges are probably wide enough to permit careful parking. Pick up the directions at point 3. This would reduce the walk to about three miles.

This walk is a sequel to No.5 in that it takes us among larger granite quarries and provides a bird's-eye view of one which is still being worked; but I must admit that my main reason for including it is the memorable view to the east. From the very outset that view is breathtaking, but as you climb towards Goonhingey it improves with each step you take. Beyond Goonhingey a different scene opens up, this time mainly towards the north; and then just beyond Roskrow and for the rest of the walk it's a return to the coastal and harbour views that we began with. This is, therefore, a walk you should save for a day of very good visibility. Ideally, choose a dry spell, too, because several patches are liable to be muddy. The nearest pub and shops are in Mabe village.

The start-and-end point is Trenoweth Wesleyan Chapel (SW 758341), on the road westwards from Mabe village to Longdowns. To drive there from Truro, take the A39 Falmouth road as far as the double roundabout at Treluswell; continue ahead on the A394, and at the second part of the next double roundabout turn left into Mabe. At the crossroads in the centre of the village turn right. Trenoweth chapel is on the left after about a quarter of a mile. Roadside parking should be possible there, and there is a small parking space behind the chapel - but if the weather is at all windy, bear in mind the notice warning about falling slates. The last mile-or-so of the walk returns along the same route as at the start, so you might find it helpful to make a few mental notes on the outward trip to help prevent you from going astray later!

1 Cross the road with care: it's not very busy as a rule, but the traffic tends to be fast. Climb the stile opposite the chapel. The path begins on top of the hedge for a few yards, then continues down on the left side. Go through the metal gate at the top of the field and then turn left. Continue on this track as it curves around the edge of a deep quarry, with a tall wire fence on your right bearing yellow warning signs. (For a note on granite quarrying in mid-Cornwall, see Walk 5.) Eventually you get a good view into the quarry itself. This is Carnsew Quarry (*). The name apparently means "Carn of the fairies", but somehow I have the impression that the fairies have departed! Soon you will reach an entrance gate with a black square attached to it. From there, follow the narrow downhill path on the left, which takes you over a small stream and brings you to the A394 Truro-Helston road.

2 Cross the road WITH EXTREME CARE and turn left. Keep to the verge, however soggy it may be after rains, and however many rusty drink-cans, broken bottles and cigarette-packets may have been deposited on it by the thoughtful occupants of passing vehicles. Luckily, you have to put up with only about a hundred yards of this before crossing a stile on your right, at the corner of a field. (Watch out for this - it's easily missed.) Cross the centre of the field, go through or over gates either side of a track and continue in the same direction to a bent gate at the top left-hand corner of the next field. (Don't forget to pause for a while hereabouts to enjoy the fine view behind, which includes sea-cliffs and Falmouth town and harbour, with St Mawes and Pendennis Castles and St Anthony lighthouse, as well as the nearby quarry.) If you'd prefer not to climb the gate, there is a rudimentary stile a

CARNSEW QUARRY

In a letter I had from Mrs Joyce Green of the Stithians Local History Group, she wrote, "I think that it is so sad to see the beautiful granite of Carnsew Quarry - which is said to be the finest granite in the country - being crushed and used to make new roads." An article by Peter Stanier in JTS No. 13 gives a detailed history of the leading granite-quarrying firm, John Freeman & Sons, which leased or owned at least eighty-seven quarries in Constantine, Stithians and Mabe parishes, though not all of them were active at any one time. Each had its number, and Carnsew is a combination of Nos. 6, 31 and 81. No. 31, the main quarry, was expanded in the 1880s, when new types of steam-powered rock drills and cranes were used here for the first time. 400 yards north of the quarry was a waterwheel which drained it by means of a pump and flat-rods (defined in the MTP's very useful glossary as "Reciprocating iron rods which were used to transfer power from a steam-engine or water-wheel to a remote location"). Here and there one or two "stillens" survive; these are raised walls built to carry the tramways which took waste to the tips. "Among the largest quarries in the district," writes Mr Stanier, "Carnsew was known for its fine-grained granite for engineering, said to be the best in Cornwall and comparable with De Lank on Bodmin Moor."

little to the right of it, but that involves a bit of scrambling, and the rough path beyond it may be rather overgrown. Turn right on the minor road and continue on that for about four hundred yards.

3 Cross the stile on the left, which has a low wooden fence on the far side, and walk up the field to a small gate in a barbed-wire fence. (Maybe you'll have more success than I did in undoing the chain on this gate; I gave up and climbed the wooden fences a few yards to the left, which surround a small reservoir.) Continue to the top-left corner of the next field and then keep by the hedge on your left, crossing four more stiles - I was glad of my wellies at the second one! - before reaching another road.

4 Turn left then immediately right, passing "Treetops". The plantation of trees has flourished surprisingly well on this hilltop, and now provides effective shelter in which other plants - and people - can flourish. As you emerge from the trees, a new panorama comes into view. In the middle distance is Stithians Church (see Walk 8). The most obvious hill on the skyline, with an engine house (Pennance) silhouetted on its left side, is Carn Marth; further right is another prominent engine house, North Treskerby; in the far distance to the right of that is St Agnes Beacon; then come United Downs and the modern Wheal Jane.

5 Take the first track on the right, about a quarter of a mile beyond "Treetops"; it passes a cottage and then several low buildings that would present an interesting challenge to the home handyman. The name of this area is Gonorman Downs (*). The track becomes a rather muddy path between hedges and then reverts to being a wider track before reaching a road. (You have now arrived at point 4 in Walk 9, so if you're feeling energetic you could slot that walk in.)

GONORMAN DOWNS

The "norman" part of this name means "nine stones" (Cornish, *nawmen)*, and almost certainly refers to an ancient stone circle or alignment; the fact that there seems to be no sign of one is hardly surprising in view of the usefulness of such stones for building. (I have heard it said that there would probably be plenty of such monuments on Carn Marth, for instance, had it not been for the Redruth and Chasewater Railway, which offered what was then - the mid-1820s - the princely sum of a shilling each for roughly-shaped granite blocks to be used as "setts".) The number nine may have had a religious or magical significance for the makers of stone circles and alignments: there is a "Nine Stones" circle on Bodmin Moor, for instance, and "Nine Maidens" can be found on the slopes of Carnmenellis and St Breock Downs. The latter does in fact have nine stones, but according to CN "Nine Maidens" is derived from the Cornish *ni meyn,* holy stones, and has nothing to do with numbers or girls. The first syllable of "Gonorman" is from the Cornish *goon,* downland, and all around this area are names that include it: Goonvean (*byghan,* small), Chywoon (*chy,* house) and Goonhingey (*hensy,* ancient house, ruin, remains). The last one seems to confirm that it was a district favoured by early man.... and Tremenhere (Walk 8) is only about half a mile from Gonorman.

6 Turn right on the road, passing Laity Moor Methodist Chapel. To continue Walk 6, at the T-junction go straight on over a stile, following the footpath sign. (But in February 1991 the field ahead had been ploughed and no attempt had been made to reinstate the path; if it is too muddy or too thickly planted for comfortable walking, you could keep to the road, turning right at the T-junction and then first left.) The path goes across the centre of the field, continuing the line of the road you came along and eventually joining the left-hand hedge near the top of the slope. Continue beside the hedge and through the gate to the road.

7 Turn left. The road curves prettily down into a lightly wooded valley with a tiny stream, and then climbs gently to Roskrow (*). After Roskrow Barton farm and some newly-converted barns you come to Roskrow itself.

8 At that point turn right on to a surfaced lane, following a footpath sign. At the farm buildings keep straight on, through or over the right-hand (wooden) gate, continuing beside the fence and over another wooden gate, where climbing has been made awkward by wire fencing. From here the footpath goes across the centre of the field to the top right-hand corner and then doubles back to reach the small wooden gate with the chain, mentioned in point 3, so that's the way you ought to go, but I suspect that the farmer, as well as yourself, would prefer you to take the direct route. From here, return to the starting-point using the route by which you came, as described in points 1 to 3.

ROSKROW

The name, often spelt "Roscrow", is pronounced to rhyme with "how", and means something like "the hut on the high downland"; Oliver Padel suggests that *goon* may have replaced an older Cornish word, *ros,* of almost identical meaning. Roskrow nowadays is perhaps too well wooded for you to be aware of the "high downland", but the view you get soon after passing it confirms the aptness of that part of the name. Roskrow Hill is, in fact, at 586 feet the highest point in St Gluvias parish. Any resemblance of Roskrow house to a hut, however, is hard to detect. A.L.Rowse mentions Roscrow in *Tudor Cornwall* as a place where the mine-owner William Carnsew stayed overnight in February 1577. The previous night he spent at Trerice and the following one at Clowance, so that puts Roskrow in fairly exalted company. According to LPH, during the reign of Henry VI it came into the possession of the Killigrews, and later belonged to the Pendarves family. The last in that line to own it was Alexander Pendarves, seven times MP for Penryn; Polsue gives very detailed treatment to that gentleman's second wife, Mary, who after Alexander's death corresponded for several years with Jonathan Swift, and in old age became famous in a small way as the inventor of a type of flower-collage. Following its Pendarves period, Roskrow came into the hands of yet another of Cornwall's leading families, the Bassets.

STITHIANS RESERVOIR AND THE ROSE-MANOWES "HOT ROCKS" SITE

WALK 7

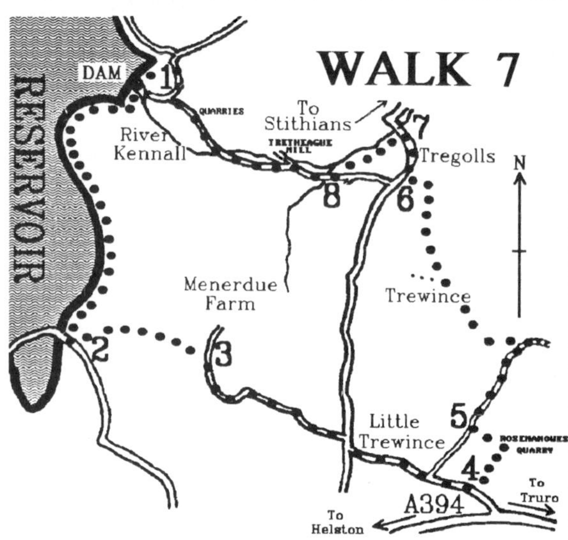

Under five miles

Points of special interest on this walk, in connection with the theme of Cornish industry old and new, include a disused watermill, several farms, a dam built to a design unique in England, and a former granite quarry which in 1977 was chosen as a pioneering site for "hot dry rocks" research. Looked on purely as a walk, it is pleasantly varied, with a lakeside section, undulating farmland and a pretty valley. Stithians Reservoir, the largest in West Cornwall, supports many wintering and migrating birds; there are (to quote MTP), "good populations of wildfowl particularly wigeon, teal and tufted duck, together with over 4,000 waders, notably golden plover and lapwing." "Large areas of mud and shallow water during the time of the autumn migration (July through October) have made this the most important inland area for migrant waders in the county." (BCIS) Some road walking is involved, but very little on roads that carry much traffic. The paths around Stithians are mostly well maintained (the village has a keen and active Ramblers group), but there are a few sections which are likely to be distinctly soggy, and others that may be rather overgrown. There is no pub on the route, and the only shop is at Tregolls Valley Nursery, a farm shop that sells fruit; several shops and a good pub are quite close to the route, in Stithians.

The walk starts at the car park beside Stithians Dam and Reservoir (*). To drive there, leave Truro on the Falmouth road (A39) and take the first right turning after the Norway Inn, then first left and first left again. This brings you to the A393 just north of Ponsanooth. At the crossroads continue ahead towards Stithians. Take the second minor road on the right, signposted to Trewithen Moor and Redruth; ignore the next two right turnings, and on reaching Stithians continue ahead with the church on your left. After about another half-mile turn sharp-left for the dam.

1 Begin by going through the gate at the end of the dam and walking across it. The hill almost straight ahead, with a mast on top, is Carnmenellis (*). Cross the wall by means of the steps at the far end of the dam and follow the

STITHIANS DAM AND RESERVOIR

The possibility of building a dam in the upper Kennall valley was considered in 1945; nearly twenty years later, work began, and in 1967 Stithians dam and treatment works were officially opened. The "arch" design meant that the central section of the dam could be thinner and therefore less costly than the "mass-gravity" type normally used in England; even so, the 800-foot-long dam, which is 140 feet high from the foundations at the centre, consumed 46,000 cubic yards of concrete. When full - a rare event these days - the reservoir covers 270 acres, is 62 feet deep at the deepest point and holds 1,190 million gallons of water. I have taken these bare facts from an article by C.B.Bainbridge, published in the *Cornish Magazine* of June 1964, and from ASI No.2 (see the note on Stithians in Walk 8); more memorable are the accounts in the latter article of the families whose lives were disrupted and whose homes and farms were destroyed. Photographs are included of four farmhouses that were demolished, and of the old bridge at Carnvullock, now probably too deeply submerged ever to be seen again except by divers, although the drought of 1990 uncovered much of the valley-bottom, and I saw a man taking his dog for a walk across another long-lost bridge over a long-lost stream.

One of the massive concrete abutments of the Stithians dam under construction. The arched central section was later joined to this.

path which runs among gorse bushes to the right. At first there are two paths beside the reservoir, but later just one. When I did this walk, in October 1990, this southern end of the reservoir had completely dried out, revealing walls, gate-posts and a bridge which probably had not been seen since the valley was flooded. After nearly a mile, a metal gate brings you to a road.

CARNMENELLIS

In previous centuries it was often spelt "Carn Menelez". "The rocky hill of the corn sheaves" (Padel) seems a rather unlikely name in view of this great granite outcrop's bleak, windswept slopes. Dexter's explanation, "carn of built stone," is more apt even if less sound linguistically: witness the following description by Michael Tangye. "With the exception of the hill summit, the 'moorstone' or surface granite has been cleared, and used for the construction of tall dry-built stone hedges, often of immense proportions, surrounding small enclosures. At the summit, granite-built cairns, probably of Bronze Age date, survive near an area where Iron Age material has also been found." (CA No. 12, 1973) At 800 feet (827 according to WG) it is taller than either Carn Brea or Carn Marth, and it ought to offer some splendid walking, but so far as I know there is no public right of way to the top.

2 Turn left, and after about fifty yards cross the four-stepped granite stile on the left. Keep by the hedge on your left, at the corner go through the wrought-iron gate, cross the stile and continue beside the wall on the right. After two more stiles you are on a cart-track.

3 At the T-junction go right along a drive or minor road, concreted at first and tarmacked beyond the bridge. At the end of that turn right on the slightly busier road, then almost immediately left, past Little Trewince farm and Rosevean. By now you will probably be able to hear the busy traffic on the A394 ahead. Just before you would have reached that, you will come to the main entrance to what was once Rosemanowes Quarry, now the Rosemanowes Research Site for the Camborne School of Mines' Geothermal Energy Project (*).

4 Turn left here. The shelter on the right affords a view of the drilling rigs in the quarry, and displays details of the history of the project, together with explanatory diagrams and photographs and an up-to-date progress report. (As explained in the boxed note, the future of the project was under threat from financial cuts at the time I was writing this, so it's quite possible that if and when I get round to writing *A Third View from Carn Marth* I'll have to put the previous sentence into the past tense.) Continue down the curving road, and just before the barrier go up the steepish, narrow path on the left, then down, through a gap in a fence, along a grassy path which looks as if it could get overgrown in summer, and through a metal farm gate.

5 Turn right, past the sign for Rosemanowes Farm. After about a quarter of a mile the drive turns quite sharply right shortly before the farm buildings; here go left, crossing a low stile just beyond a black metal farm gate. Walk fairly close to the wall on the right, but keep straight on where the wall curves right, and about fifty yards further on cross the stile on the right. Now go straight on up to Trewince farm. The track is wide but may well be overgrown: when I walked it, it had quite recently been cleared, but young and very virulent nettles were springing up enthusiastically. Another hazard,

ROSEMANOWES GEOTHERMAL ENERGY RESEARCH SITE

The radioactive elements in the granite deep under Cornwall, which are presumably associated with the problem of radon gas, also create dry heat, and at Rosemanowes experiments are being carried out to try to convert this heat into useful energy. The method involves drilling pairs of wells; water is pumped down one, passes through natural fractures in the hot rock ("enhanced" with explosives and by the use of a water-based gel), and - at least in theory - emerges at a high temperature from the other. Work began in 1977, and the progress of the research since then has been recorded in a series of interesting pamphlets (copies of the 1987 one were available at the site when I was there), as well as in the display in the observation building. Results have, on the whole, been encouraging, but the work so far has cost £33 million, and it is estimated that to continue the project by drilling four miles down, as the scientists say is necessary, will require a further £50 million. On the right is part of an item from the *West Briton* of 10th January 1991. Early in February it was announced that only £3 million would be made available to cover the next three years, so it seems almost certain that the work-force will have to be cut and underground work discontinued until further notice.

'Hot Rocks closed' claims denied

A CLAIM this week that the Government had abandoned the Camborne School of Mines, geothermal energy (hot rocks) project, was described as "pure speculation", by the Department of Energy.

The claim was made in "The Guardian", on Tuesday. A Department spokeswoman said that while all renewable energy projects were being reviewed, no decisions had yet been taken.

"A review of all renewable energy technologies has been under way for about a year and the full position will be announced soon," she added.

In fact, the decision had been expected at the end of November and all 60 employees at the project base in Rosemanowes Quarry, Long Downs, are anxiously awaiting the announcement.

especially towards the top, is boggy conditions: I had the impression that in wet spells the footpath doubles as the bed of a stream. (Moral: sandals and bare legs are not ideal gear for this walk!) Turn left among the farm buildings, go through two metal gates, over a cattle-grid, and then turn right immediately. Walk with the wall (or hedge: in Cornwall the terms are almost interchangeable) on your right for a few yards, then pass through another gate and continue in the same direction, heading towards Stithians church, with the wall on your left now. Cross the impressive stile at the corner of the field; you are back on the right side of the wall again till you cross another stile (steps in a wall), after which the path runs between hedges.

6 At the road (which can be busy, so please take care) turn right, past the Tregolls Valley Nursery, where Mr and Mrs Barter run a farm shop, open every day except winter Sundays.

7 Just beyond the greenhouses and before the bridge, take the signed footpath on the left,which stays quite near the stream, and crosses three stiles.

8 At the road turn right and cross the bridge to Tretheague Mill (*), where the water that once supplied power for the wheel now rushes down a bank. Ignore the track on the left just before the building; go up the hill and continue along this well-made path with the Kennall valley on your left. Soon the dam comes into view, and the path runs uphill between hedges. At the road turn right past the water treatment plant to return to the car park.

TRETHEAGUE AND OTHER NEARBY MILLS

Tretheague was the second of the "nearly 40 water wheels" turned by "the little river Kennal" according to Lake's *Parochial History of Cornwall* (1869). The first mill on the river was Carn Mill, below Carnmeasure. Less than a mile downstream is Tregonning Mill, with its recently restored wheel, very unusual in Cornwall because it is a "breast-shot" one - that is, the water was fed to it half-way up rather than at the top or bottom. (Some details - not all of them accurate - and a photograph of Tregonning are included in CW under the name Stithians Mill, and there is an article about it in ASI No.4.) Tregonning was a three-storey corn mill, but Tretheague had two floors, with the grinding stones on the upper floor and the machinery below. It takes its name from the farm it served, now dominated by an imposing Georgian mansion which is on the shorter route of Walk 8. The name possibly means "farm full of riches" or "beautiful farm".

Stithians dam and reservoir, with Carnmenellis in the distance

1. Near Goodern, February 1991. (Walk 1)

2. Inside the ruined power house of the old Wheal Jane. (Walk 1)

3. Gwennap Pit, with Carn Marth in the distance. (Walk 2)

4. Brunton arsenic calciner at Wheal Busy. In the distance can be seen the engine house and smithy of Great Wheal Busy. (Walk 2)

5. The lambreth flue leading to the stack at Wheal Busy arsenic works. (Walk 2)

6. The Poldice arsenic works. In the distance are the engine houses of Wheal Unity Wood and Killifreth. (Walk 2)

7. The shadow of one of the engine houses at Wheal Unity Wood points towards the Hawke's Shaft engine house, Killifreth. (Walk 2)

8. The startling colours created by mineral deposits in the Mount Wellington tailings dam. In the distance are the clock tower and ruined engine houses of Consols copper mine. (Walk 3)

9/10. The elegant stack of the Cornwall Arsenic Company Works at Bissoe, before and after the lightning struck. (Walk 3)

11. The bob wall of Nangiles Mine's pumping engine house, overlooking the Carnon Valley. (Walk 4)

12/13 Two views of Argal reservoir on a January morning. The church is that of Mabe. (Walk 5)

14. Sunset at Restronguet Creek, February 1991. In the background are the woods of Carclew; part of Devoran Quay is in the middle distance; and closer are the remains of embankments created by tin-streamers about two centuries ago. (Walk 11)

15/16. Granite quarries near Mabe. (Walk 5)

17/18 The River Kennall near Polkinhorne's mill. (Walk 8)

19. The remains of a pair of incorporating mills at the Kennall Gunpowder Works. (Walk 9)

20. A spring day at Kennall Vale. (Walk 9)

21. Perran Foundry, March 1991. The building in the middle distance, originally the Foundry's New Pattern Shop, was converted during the early 1890s into a three-storey corn and grist mill, and the launder shown in the photograph was built to carry water from the south leat to drive a new 22-foot overshot waterwheel. (Walk 10)

22. Restronguet Creek, looking downstream from the Carnon Stream Mine. (Walk 11)

23. Calenick Creek as seen from the former Newham branch line. (Walk 12)

24. The weir and sluice gates on the River Kenwyn, near Carvedras, Truro. In the background is the modern railway viaduct, with "Brunel's stumps" beside it. (Walk 12)

25. The open-air theatre in a quarry on Carn Marth, March 1991. (Walk 14)

26. The flooded quarry at the top of Carn Marth......and a small part of The View! (Walk 14)

WALK 8

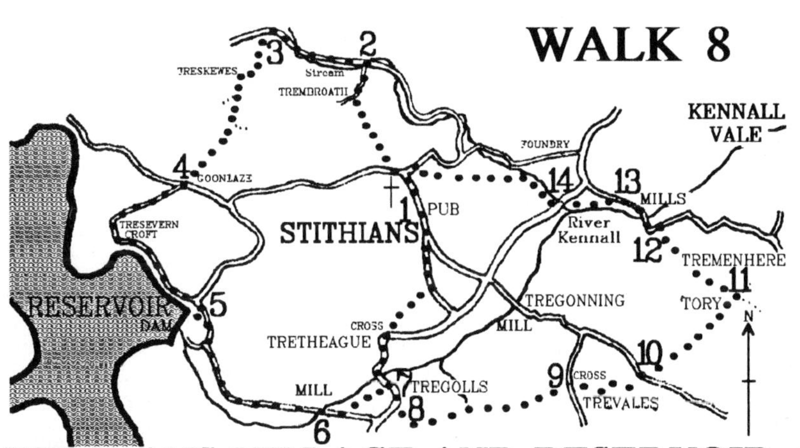

STITHIANS VILLAGE AND RESERVOIR, WITH A POSSIBLE EXTENSION TO THE KENNALL VALE

Under four miles, or a little over six miles if you include Tremenhere and the upper part of the Kennall Vale.
Can be linked to Walks 7 and 9.

This is an enjoyable walk through typical Cornish farming country, but to do it - especially the longer version - you need to be reasonably fit (able, for example, to climb high, awkward stiles and rickety gates) and equipped with stout, waterproof footwear. But please don't conclude that this is an assault course requiring commando training: a few little local difficulties serve to enhance your sense of achievement when you get back to the Seven Stars. Certainly that's how we felt as we settled down by the fire on the January day when we walked it. Among the many attractions on the walk are several streams and small rivers in pretty valleys, the man-made lake and dam, at least two former watermills, two old Cornish crosses (one on each route), an ancient standing-stone and the village of Stithians itself, with its fine church. If you would like to look inside the church, ring the Rev. Michael Warner (0209-860123) to arrange to pick up the key; the vicarage is close to the church, on the north side. The farm shop at Tregolls is on the longer route and very close to the shorter one; Stithians has several shops, the Seven Stars ("Welcoming feel to this comfortable local inn," as David Guthrie remarks in CGCP), and public toilets opposite the pub. You could make an all-day walk of it by slotting in Walk 7 when you get to the dam; when you reach Tregolls (point 6 in that walk), pick up the directions for the longer version of this walk again at point 7; and then at point 12 you could turn right on the road and visit the CTNC site at Kennall Vale as described in Walk 9. If you are very energetic, of course, you could add the whole of Walk 9, bringing the grand total to about thirteen miles; to do that, turn right just beyond Tory (point 11 in this walk), picking up the route of Walk 9 towards the end of point 3 and visiting the Kennall Vale site before returning to Stithians.

This walk starts and ends in Stithians village (*), where plenty of roadside parking is usually available between the church and the pub. Directions for driving there from Truro are given for the previous walk; when you reach the church, turn left.

1 Walk back to the church and turn left along Hendra Road. The large building on the corner, opposite the church, was once the vicarage, and became the Stithians Hotel; I have vivid memories of overeating at the Carvery there, back in the 1970s. A notice at the gate now says "Hotel All Closed Down." There is an old cross in its garden, and another in the churchyard, at the east end of the church. After a short distance, turn right on to the footpath signed to Trembroath, crossing a stone cattle-grid. The path, which is very clearly defined and even paved for part of its length, takes you over three more cattle-grids or low stiles before you reach a minor road at Chyvounder ("the house in the lane") and Trembroath. The hill with a mast on it which was ahead as you came along the path is Carnkie (said to rhyme with tie), just north of Four Lanes, and to the right of that is Carn Marth. Turn right on the minor road (in fact, you continue in more-or-less the same direction).

2 This joins a slightly more important-looking road at a bridge over a wide stream; here turn left. This is a very attractive part of the walk: the road runs beside the stream, which is crossed by a little clapper bridge; later there is a small weir, and at the point where the road crosses the stream I half-expected to find another old watermill, but I have not come across any reference to one there. Next the road curves left and crosses another bridge.

3 Immediately after that, cross the stile on the left, beside a gate marked Treskewes Farm. ("Treskewes", or "Treskewis" according to the OS map, means "the farm at the place of the elder trees".) The path crosses yet another bridge and runs beside a small stream below a short terrace of cottages; it then becomes a farm track and passes through the farmyard. Its "official" course is slightly blocked here, and the owner requests that walkers turn left after passing the farmhouse, then right, between an old stone barn and a newer haybarn. At the grassy lane, turn left (but look right first for a good view of Carn Marth, easily identifiable by the quarry near the top). Where the lane curves right towards Tresevern, don't follow it but go straight on through an open gateway with a blocked stile on the left side. Walk beside the hedge on the left and cross the quite high stile ahead, but ignore the one

STITHIANS

The history of this village and its surroundings is unusually well documented, because it has a very active Local History Group, which produced a book called *Aspects of History in Stithians* in 1980 and has added another volume in alternate years ever since; so far, every one has managed to live up to the claim, "Always Something Interesting". From now on I shall refer to the series simply as *Aspects.* I have found particularly useful issues 2 and 4, which have sections about watermills, quarries and the making of the dam and reservoir. The publication of each new issue is timed to coincide with the Stithians Show, which has been held every July (on the Monday following the Sunday closest to 13th) since 1834, apart from the periods of the two World Wars, and has achieved a status unrivalled in the county by any agricultural show apart from the Royal Cornwall Show itself. The showground includes the Playing Field beside the Seven Stars, together with some adjoining fields belonging to Ennis and Carbis Farm. Since 1929, one of the features of the Show has been performances by the Stythians Silver Band, whose high standards have won them many awards "up-country" as well as in Cornwall. If you can get hold of a copy of *Aspects* No.4, try a walk around the village with Sydney J. Bowden's entertaining though, sadly, uncompleted article, "A Stroll through Stithians' Past" as your guide. The parish church itself was dealt with very cursorily by Charles Henderson in his *Cornish Church Guide* (1925): "This is a 15th century church in a granite country, and has been swept empty of all its interesting contents." I cannot challenge him on the matter of its contents, since I have never managed to find the church unlocked, but others have found much more to say about the building and its history: see, for example, Arthur Mee's *Cornwall* (1937), which refers to "the grand tower, which has stood 500 years, one of the noblest granite towers in Cornwall", and also to "the massive granite font"; *The Story of St Stythians Parish Church in Cornwall* (1948) by William Cumber; an article in *Aspects,* Volume 3; and the church guide written by the present vicar and published in 1990. The last of these includes an interesting "development plan" showing the alterations to the building from the "Celtic Cell" of about the 6th century to the Victorian restoration by the notorious J. P. St Aubyn ("merciless", according to John Betjeman); there is also a vivid drawing showing the likely arrangement of galleries, box pews and sash windows in the late 18th century. The church was dedicated to "St Stedyana" in 1301, thus giving rise to much contention among the scholars as to who this saint could have been; among the contenders are St Etaine (Irish), St Swithin (from Wessex), St Stinan (Welsh), St Diana (!) and St Stephen alias St Etienne (Breton).

on the left immediately after that. The hill ahead now is Carnmenellis: see the note in Walk 7. You have to cross two more high stiles, the second of which is quite awkward because of a missing step on the far side. Now the path runs near the edge of a small copse and then diverges to the right among the trees before passing through the row of cottages at Goonlaze ("green down") to the road.

4 Turn right, then immediately fork left along a minor road which ends at Tresevern House. Here take the lane on the left, which runs beside Stithians Reservoir - again, see the note in Walk 7. The lane is used by tractors or other heavy vehicles, and is likely to be very muddy. After about half a mile it curves behind a bungalow and reaches a road.

5 Turn right into the car park beside the dam, and follow the tarmacked road on the left that curves down towards the water treatment works. Just before the entrance gate to that, turn left on the rough lane that runs down the valley of the Kennall river. Up on the left near the start are some old quarries. Roughly half a mile further on, the sound of rushing water in an old leat announces Tretheague Mill, the subject of another note in Walk 7.

6 Just beyond the bridge, cross the stile on the left; there is a footpath sign. This is another part of the walk where you will probably encounter mud. The path, which crosses several stiles, keeps quite close to the stream, and eventually brings you to a road. (Take care here: it is more likely to be busy than most of the others on this route.)

7 AT THIS POINT YOU HAVE TO CHOOSE BETWEEN THE SHORTER AND LONGER ROUTES. For the longer one, via Tremenhere, which provides a possible link to the Kennall Vale gunpowder works site and the rest of Walk 9, read on from the start of the next-but-one paragraph.

TO RETURN DIRECT TO STITHIANS, turn left, past the mansion of Tretheague, typically Georgian in its strict symmetry but perhaps less so in its battlements. The road in front of it is sunken, almost in the style of a ha-ha. Notice the fine old Cornish cross, up on the bank beside the main entrance to the house. Henderson and Coates in OCBS (1928), presumably refer to the nearby bridge and this cross when they write, "Tretheage Bridge .... is very picturesque with two square openings roofed by huge slabs of granite. On the island-pier, between them stood a Celtic Cross which was thrown into the river and forgotten, until rediscovered in recent years." At the corner, opposite a house called Woodside (in January 1991 - but house names tend to change, as irritated users of some of my books have reminded me!), turn left over a cattle-grid; there is a footpath sign. Don't walk beside the hedge on the left, but go uphill over the middle of the field towards the left end of the line of houses. The line of the path soon becomes clear; after a low stile it runs beside a house and reaches a road. There turn left, and soon you come down to the main street, the Seven Stars and the church. Opposite the pub and playing field formerly stood Crellow House in its extensive grounds; see the note on Tresavean Mine in Walk 13.

FOR THE LONGER WALK, turn right, past the Tregolls Valley Nursery, and take the signed footpath (a farm track)on the left where the road bends right.

8 Just before you reach the house, turn left through a wooden gate (not the metal one closer to the house). I say "through" the gate, but in fact we were unable to open it, and it was almost too rickety to climb: a hint of what proved to be true, that the path beyond is less well maintained than most in the Stithians area. Keep beside the hedge on the right. The first stile, close to a double gate, consists of steps in quite a high wall, made the more awkward to climb by gorse. Immediately beyond the second stile, don't miss the third one, on the right: again rather awkward, but not as bad as the first. Next, go diagonally across the field to some rusty remains of gates, again in too dilapidated a state to open or climb easily. Continue in the same line down to the boggy area in the corner of the field. On the right-hand side of this wet patch, a few rough stepping stones help you to cross the sluggish stream; then climb up on the bank and go left along the top of it, over a water-pipe, and then across a little bridge and over the hedge beyond. At this point - at least in mid-winter, when we walked it - another bridge is needed, or at least stepping stones; but somehow we managed to scramble around the pool or stream and across the remaining bogland, or "moor" as it is commonly known in Cornwall, without getting wet feet. Still continue in roughly the same direction as you were going before reaching the moor, not up either of the obvious tracks but beside the line of gorse bushes on the left. Keep left of the pool in what looks like a small quarry, and go on in the same line across the next field, through a gap and then just to the left of the pylon, followed by a contraption which we presumed was designed to hold a cow. The muddy lane beyond that brings you to a gate (another one that has to be climbed) and a road.

9 Here a very short diversion to the left is worthwhile, to see the ancient Cornish cross in a field on the right; but to continue the walk, turn right and then left along the surfaced entrance drive to Trevales Farm. Go through the farmyard and straight on via a wooden gate. Soon you will reach a duck pond; keep left of that. The next section of the path was extremely soggy in January: almost part of the stream, in fact! Finally there's one more rusty gate to climb, and this brings you to another minor road. From here on, you may be relieved to know, the going is comparatively straightforward.

10 Continue straight ahead, following the bridleway sign, along this pleasant lane between hedges. The next metal gate actually opens! So does the wooden one that follows, and this brings you to the nicely renovated farmhouse at Tory, with its unaggressive geese and its pigeons busily popping in and out of holes in the nearby barn. The fish-pond apparently originated as a millpool: the 1906 OS map shows a waterwheel at Tory; in 1920 this was supplying domestic electricity. The horseshoes on the gateposts may be a token that the house is old; whether its name is Cornish or political I don't know.

11 Immediately after crossing the cattle grid, take the signed footpath on the left. Cross to the field corner (not quite in the direction indicated by the footpath sign), crossing a stile with a gate in front of it, and then a second stile as you approach Tremenhere Farm; the standing stone or menhir which gives the farm its name is on the right here. Presumably it dates from the early Bronze Age, but my books on Cornish archaeology give no details. The next stile is at the field corner, near the farm buildings; cattle had churned the area around it into a morass in January, so we had to climb on to the wall at a different point. The path continues in the same direction as before, towards Stithians church, so go down the wall-steps on the left rather than the ones which lead to the farmhouse. After the well-made stile with steps, continue in the same line across the field and through a gate to the road. On the right here is the very attractively restored terrace of cottages known as Little Plymouth. Mrs Joyce Green of the Stithians Local History Group tells me that in the field opposite, where a lake is being made, "is a bunch of trees, said to be a burial ground after a battle."

12 Here, unless you have plans to visit the Kennall Vale gunpowder works site on another occasion, a very worthwhile diversion would be to turn right and go there now; it would add about three miles to the walk. For directions, see the earlier part of Walk 9. But to return to Stithians, turn left. Soon a bridge (colour picture 17) takes you across the River Kennall or Kennal ("Kennell" according to Sheila Bird and "Kinnall" to John Betjeman) to the interesting old buildings which were once Polkinhorne's corn mill, complete with Victorian letter-box. There were formerly three mills within 200 yards of each other on this part of the river, including the Kennal Paper Mills (*), the remains of which are a little way downstream on private land. Next for a while the road runs beside the river (colour picture 18); then it curves away uphill.

KENNAL PAPER MILLS

The History Group's second book has interesting details about these mills and the processes involved in paper making. Records show that they were active by 1809 and still operating in 1851, but had closed as paper mills by 1910. In 1908 they were described as corn mills. The Kennal mills made paper of "superior quality", mainly from rags, which "arrived at the mill in bales. They were shredded, pulped in water by stamps, again powered by water from the River Kennal, and processed into paper." The mill owner in 1809, William Tucker, advertised in the local press "The following kinds of paper: thick and thin post, plain, black and gilt edge; foolscap and pot; copy and large post; blotting, blue and cartridge, whited brown and brown of all size

13 As you pass under the power-lines, cross the stile on the left, where there is a footpath sign (in need of re-erection) to Foundry. Keep by the hedge on the right and go through the kissing-gate on the edge of Stithians.

14 Turn left, and then after a few yards right on to a gravelled path with a signpost to Stithians Church. (The cottage-name, Tremenhere, is puzzling: is it linked with the farm in some way, or was there a standing stone nearby? The 1813 one-inch OS map indicates a Tremenhere just north of here, a farm known locally as "Tremenhere Skinner", in addition to the one on the walk route, and not far to the west occurs the field-name "Post Field", which is another clue to the one-time existence of a menhir.) After more stiles, a footbridge and another kissing-gate, ignore the second footbridge on the right, which leads to the area known as Foundry from the fact that it was once the site of a water-powered hammer mill ("Bryant's Foundry" on the 1813 map) where shovels were made. (The last hammer mill to survive in Cornwall was at Roseworthy, west of Camborne, which was set up about 1790 and closed in 1939. Three photographs of it are included in HCMSS, one of which shows a shovel being made.) Follow the path to the left over yet another footbridge and stile, and head just to the right of the church tower. The stiles show the way. At the road, turn left for the church and left again for the pub, toilets and shops.

Polkinhorne's Mill with the waterwheel in place - an undated photograph reproduced by courtesy of the R.I.C.

WALK 9

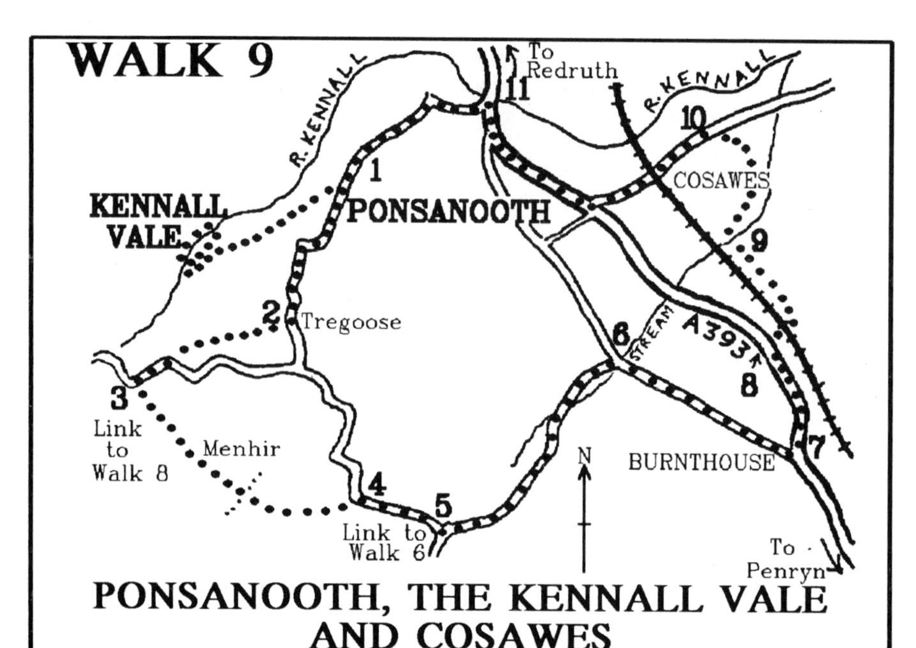

PONSANOOTH, THE KENNALL VALE AND COSAWES

Just over five miles. The Kennall Vale site could be toured separately as a stroll of a mile or less.

Having just returned from another visit to Kennall Vale, I am keener than ever to say this is a place you mustn't miss, whether your taste is for natural beauty or industrial archaeology or both. Early in March 1991, after heavy rains, it was even more dramatic than usual, with the water in full spate, not only in the river itself but in the leats above, from which it was spilling over at several points in waterfalls and cataracts. The devastating gales of February 1990 did great damage to the trees, and uprooted stumps are still everywhere to be seen; here and there the trees have in their fall dislodged granite blocks in buildings or the side walls of leats; but the Cornwall Trust for Nature Conservation are planting saplings, and new plant-growth is starting to flourish where more light has been admitted. One small consolation for the loss of trees is that some of the impressive remains of the gunpowder works are now more visible than before. I have suggested parking near the Vale so that you could conveniently explore it either as part of the full walk or on a separate occasion. The rest of the route, parts of which overlap Walks 6 and 8, includes several other points of interest, notably Cosawes, the site of an earlier gunpowder works; an impressive railway viaduct in another beautiful part of the Kennall valley, close to which was an old tin mine; and the village of Ponsanooth, which has many attractive and interesting features, probably unsuspected by at least 95% of the motorists who hasten through. It is quite an easy walk, but likely to be muddy, especially around Tremenhere Farm and in the Kennall Vale. I was unable to avoid including two short stretches of main road, one of them in Ponsanooth. A pub and shop are very conveniently placed near the end of the route in Ponsanooth.

To drive to Ponsanooth from Truro, take the A39 south towards Falmouth. After about six miles, watch for the Norway Inn on the right, and nearly a mile beyond that fork right by a sign advertising "Cosawes Park Homes". After about another mile this road brings you to the edge of Ponsanooth. Turn right on to the main road (A393) and drive through the village. On reaching the post office / store (on the left just before the bridge), turn left. The entrance to the Kennall Vale, which is the start-point for the walk directions, is on the right about half a mile up this road, almost opposite Cotwood Cottage. Although people do park beside the road just beyond the entrance, it is very narrow there, and parking is much more practicable a few hundred yards further back, opposite an estate road called Forth an Cos, or on the side road a few yards up the hill from there (Kennall Park / Cot Wood).

The site of the Kennall Gunpowder Works (*) is now leased to the CTNC and is open to the public (except on the fourth Monday in February each year). Dogs MUST be kept on leads. In a sense, this is really a detour on the walk, and you could leave it out if time is short; but if you do, be sure to come back another day and if possible allow at least a couple of hours for the visit. Directions for that are included in the boxed note.

THE KENNALL GUNPOWDER WORKS
(Colour pictures 19 & 20)

Explosives were important to the mining and granite quarrying industries, and until 1809 they had to be imported into the county. In that year a gunpowder works was set up at Cosawes .....More of that later. The Fox family, owners of the Perran Foundry (see Walk 10), were impressed by the success of Cosawes, and in 1812 they launched their own gunpowder factory here in Kennall Vale. The site was ideal, being close to the mines, roads and a potential labour force at Ponsanooth, but well screened from the latter by trees (in fact, many more trees were planted to minimise blast impact in the event of an accident, and some massive granite walls were built for the same purpose), and having an excellent power-supply in the form of the Kennall River. "This river," wrote Hitchens and Drew in their *History of Cornwall,* 1824, "from its source to its union with the sea runs about five miles and a half, in which short distance it turns thirty-nine water wheels all in active and full employ. It may be doubted, if within the same short distance another such stream can be found in England." The enterprise at Kennall Vale flourished. It began on quite a small scale at the lower end, near Kennall House, but in 1844 a new section was added above, in Roches Wood. In the 1860s it employed fifty or more men; but after that its fortunes waned along with those of the mines themselves, and the invention of dynamite and gelignite in the 1880s hastened its demise, although it did not close completely on this site till about 1914. Later, a quarry was opened near the top end, and the ruined concrete buildings near the quarry-pit, now flooded, are relics of this. Transport within the gunpowder works was by horse-and-cart. The safety-record of the works during the hundred years of existence was remarkably good. The few serious accidents were fully reported in the local press; the best-known one was caused by a spark on the clothing of a woman bringing hot food into a mixing-house.

The detailed story of the many processes involved in gunpowder manufacture, and of the Kennall Gunpowder Works in particular, is fascinating, and can be read in Bryan Earl's book, *Cornish Explosives* (Trevithick Society, 1978), and even more fully in the excellent archaeological report prepared for the CTNC in 1985-6 by John R. Smith (obtainable from The Cornwall Trust for Nature Conservation, Five Acres, Allet, Truro, TR4 9DJ; phone, 0872-73939).

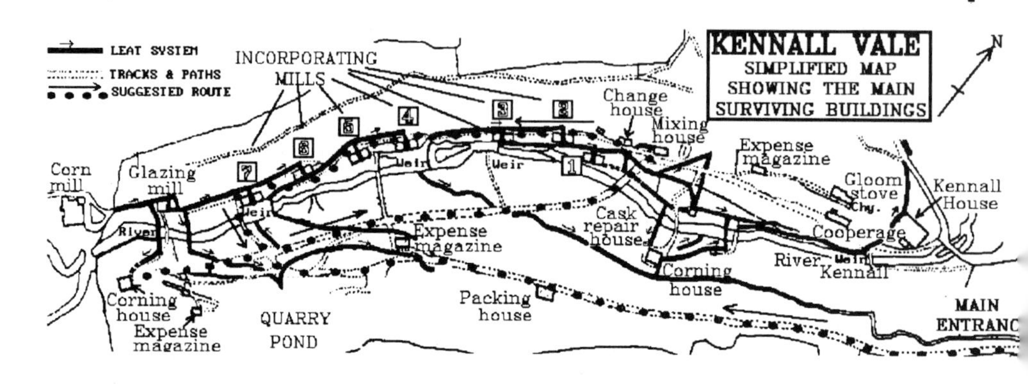

You will be able to make more sense of what you see as you walk around the site if you have some idea of the steps in the manufacturing process. In very simplified form, these were as follows: The raw materials (charcoal, saltpetre and sulphur) were mixed in a rotating wooden barrel in a Mixing House, and taken to an Incorporating Mill, where the mixture was dampened and ground to a fine powder by vertically-mounted millstones. Then it went to a Press House to be compressed into a "cake" about an inch thick; next this was broken (using wooden mallets) into lumps in a Breaking Down House, then reduced to granules in a Corning House, dried by means of piped steam in a Gloom Stove, and separated from dust in a Dusting House. Finally the granules were rounded and glazed (so that they could easily be poured into holes and were water-resistant - important in damp mine-workings) by being rotated in a drum with graphite in a Glazing Mill, before being packed in wooden crates. The "Expense Magazines" were used for storage of materials between processes. Most of these operations were powered by water-wheels, and much of the complex system of leats is still visible.

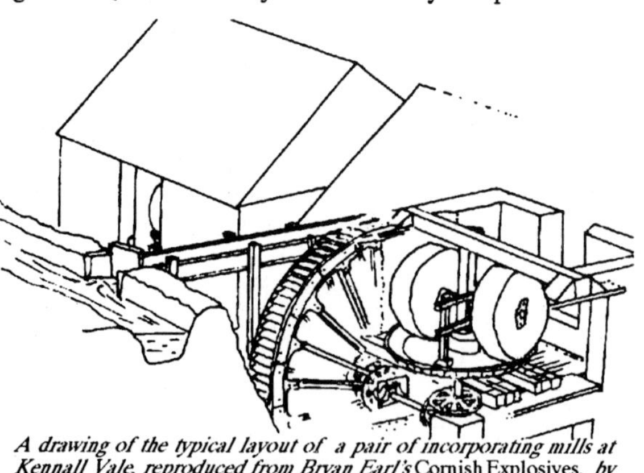

A drawing of the typical layout of a pair of incorporating mills at Kennall Vale, reproduced from Bryan Earl's Cornish Explosives, *by kind permission of the author.*

It would take another book the size of this one to give you a proper "guided tour", so all I shall attempt is to point out the main features of interest. As you walk along the path from the main entrance, you will catch glimpses of Kennall House in the valley-bottom. Most of the 1812 works was in what is now the private garden of the house, and little remains to be seen. The granite chimney is part of a Gloom Stove. After a few hundred yards, the first sizeable building on the left was a Packing House. Eight more buildings which originally stood just beyond this were destroyed when the quarry buildings were erected. (Walk to the left here to see the flooded quarry-pit, one of the scenic attractions of the Vale. See pages 134-5 for details about this quarry.) Soon afterwards, turn sharp right on to the lower track leading back down the valley, where you get a good view of some leats and blast-walls. As you cross the bridge, the large building ahead was a Mixing House; the smaller one to the left was the Change House, where the workmen changed into pocketless woollen suits. Turn left to walk up-stream. Now come the most spectacular industrial relics at Kennall Vale: the seven pairs of Incorporating Mills, each with its own leat to supply its overshot waterwheel, and each in turn a little more complete than the previous one. All of them can be entered from the upper level. The first three were part of the 1812 works; just beyond the third one (with water pouring from its leat) is a pair of grindstones, the lower one in good condition. Notice the rendering of fine cement on the insides of the mill walls, designed to prevent explosive dust from clinging to them. The roofs have all gone; for safety reasons, these would have been light, wooden structures. The gearing and ruined waterwheel in the last mill are explained on page 139. Now cross the river again by the wooden foot-bridge and turn right to see the buildings at the top of the site. The largest of these was a Corning House, and is remarkable for the pit beneath it which once held the waterwheel. Inside the building is a dis-mantled waterwheel, including cogwheels and an axle nearly two feet in diameter and about eighteen feet long. (Visible over the wall at the top end of the site is one of the corn mills mentioned in Walk 8, section 12; it still has a large waterwheel in place, but unfortunately that cannot be seen from this angle. The dismantled waterwheel in the Corning House seems likely to have been used in this building when it was a paper mill.) The walk now returns to the main entrance by the path you first came along.

Of course, there is far more here to discover. What you should do is arm yourself with John Smith's report and come back for a full day!

1 To continue the walk, go on up the road for about another half mile.

2 Just as you reach farm buildings (Tregoose) on the right, cross the stile on the right. The path - muddy in places - keeps by the hedge on the left. Notice how well the wooded valley on your right hides the gunpowder works. You cross four more stiles, all on the left of open gateways, and one last one which brings you to another road. Turn right, passing a terrace called Little Plymouth on your left. (You are now at point 12 in Walk 8, which could be slotted in now if you want a longer walk; and that in turn links with Walk 7, if you're really a glutton for punishment.)

3 At the end of the terrace, turn left up the concrete drive and climb the wall ahead by the step-stile. Now cross the field and after negotiating another stile over a wall, go down to walk on the right of the hedge (good luck with the mud!), heading towards three telegraph poles. Go over more steps on the right of a gate, and walk on with the hedge on your left. (Look over the hedge to see an ancient standing stone in the middle of the field, which explains why this farm is called Tremenhere. For comments on the evidence of prehistoric man in this area, see Walk 6, the note on Gonorman Downs, and Walk 8, section 11.) After the next stile the hedge is on your right; then another stile, following which you go slightly left to yet another stile by a telegraph pole. Continue straight on across a bridleway, keeping the hedge on your right. The next stile is rather awkward because of low, rickety metal gates on both sides. After this, bear left to a wide gap in the hedge with a farm beyond, and continue straight on to a gate which brings you to a road. (Here you join the route of Walk 6 at point 6.)

4 Turn right, passing Lidgey Farm and Laity Moor Methodist Chapel.

5 At the T-junction, turn left. This road passes Laity ("dairy") Farm, complete with duck-ponds, and is skirted by a stream for much of its length.

6 At the next T-junction, you could turn left to return quickly to Ponsanooth; but for the complete walk, turn right. Notice the stream running into the valley: we see this again later. The view on your left now includes Perranarworthal Church in a hollow and Carnon Downs on the hill beyond; Wheal Jane is on the skyline further left, and St Day on the extreme left.

7 At Burnthouse (*), on the main road, turn left. Please take great care: this is the Falmouth-Redruth road, and the traffic can be heavy and fast. Cross to face the oncoming vehicles.

8 After about a quarter of a mile, turn right by a public footpath sign on to a track between hedges, which takes you on a bridge over the Truro-Falmouth railway line (*). Immediately after this, cross the wooden stile on the left. The path runs between wire fences. Notice the older railway cutting on the right, and just before you cross the stream at the bottom there are the tumbledown remains of an old viaduct; the modern line runs on the embankment on your left. This stream is the one you walked beside near Laity Farm, and it reaches here via a culvert under the embankment. Be careful when crossing the stile, which can be slippery.

BURNTHOUSE

Several places in Cornwall and one in Devon have this name. Mabe Burnthouse is the nearest; Oliver Padel's comment on that in CPN is "*Burnthouse* is self-explanatory, but the reason is not known." Of course, the reason may be different in each case, but one possibility here could be charcoal burning in the nearby Cosawes or Burnthouse Woods, and two other explanations could be associated with Magdalen Mine, less than a mile away. "Burning houses" were employed to roast tin ore in order to drive off impurities, particularly arsenic; and a "blowing house" was an early form of smelting house. It was common practice for blowing-house owners to set fire to their thatched roofs every so often in order to retrieve the valuable minerals caught up in them from the smoke.

THE FALMOUTH BRANCH LINE

The Falmouth branch of Brunel's Cornwall Railway was opened in 1863. The piles of his original timber-topped viaduct stand beside the newer one (built about 1920) in the Kennall valley. The line originally ran a few yards further west than now, crossing the Cosawes valley on a bridge beside the modern embankment and then entering the cutting, now partly overgrown and a dumping-ground for rubbish, which runs parallel to the new one.

9 On emerging among the bungalows and mobile homes of Cosawes Country Park, turn left as directed by the sign. The footpath stays on the left side of the valley, eventually passing toilets. It then runs by a line of young fir trees, in front of a mobile home and down a slope, to reach the road via a small copse on the right. A few millstones are the only obvious evidence that the Country Park is built on the site of the Cosawes Gunpowder Works (*); there are some old buildings among the bungalows, and near the main administrative buildings is a waterwheel.

THE COSAWES GUNPOWDER WORKS

As mentioned in the first note, the valley below Cosawes Wood was the site of Cornwall's first gunpowder works (1809). Charcoal for the mixture was obtained from the wood, and the little stream was the power-source. Bryan Earl's interesting account of the Cosawes powder factory in CE indicates that the works, which probably had four incorporating mills, was a financial success at first. Production was apparently 2000 barrels of gunpowder per year, each barrel holding 100 lbs. Soon , however, Cosawes suffered because of competition from the Kennall works, whose owners bought up the smaller site by 1844. By 1870 the Cosawes buildings were used only for storage. The surviving waterwheel dates from 1893, long after the gunpowder works closed, and was used for cutting timber. The millstone at the main entrance to the Cosawes Country Park site is from one of the incorporating mills. Made of fine-grained limestone and weighing about two tons, it has (to quote Bryan Earl) "a 9.25 in. square hole through the middle for the drive bearing as well as two 1.5 in. dia. holes for the retaining plate plugs." Mr Earl refers to such stones as "runners" or "rollers", because unlike the granite millstones in corn mills they were positioned vertically and the crushing was done by the rolling circumference edge.

10 Turn left at the road (but to see the millwheel mentioned in the boxed note, go a few yards to the right first, to the main entrance to the site). Now you will see plenty of evidence of modern industry on the right; much harder to detect, on the left shortly before the viaduct, are any relics of Wheal Magdalen (*). The ruined walls here are remains of an iron foundry, shown on the 1908 O.S. map; this was part of the Perran Foundry operation (see Walk 10). The track on the right after the viaduct is private - unfortunately, because it affords splendid views of the valley and the viaduct. We have to continue along the road and turn right into Ponsanooth. Perhaps you're ready for a pub-visit by now.....but in any case, before you return to your car spare a few more minutes to look around Ponsanooth (*).

11 Walk past the Post Office and turn left just before the road bridge. Continue up this road for about half a mile to get back to the suggested parking place.

WHEAL MAGDALEN

Magdalen (pronounced *Maudlin)* Bal or Wheal Magdalen, perhaps named after a nearby chapel, was a tin mine on the northern side of Cosawes Wood. Evidence exists that it was working by 1522, and a plan dated 1730 shows 17 shafts. MMC gives the mine's history in detail and has interesting photographs from the 1920s showing, among other things, the old motor-car engine that was used for hoisting. A photograph from about 1913 showing stamps at Magdalen driven by a water turbine is published in MC.

PONSANOOTH

The name is often explained as "new bridge", but Oliver Padel in CPN says it means "bridge of the water-course" or possibly "goose bridge". In Ponsanooth during the early days of Wheal Magdalen there was a blowing house (for smelting tin) with stamping mill. This made use of water-power from the Kennall, like most of Ponsanooth's industry of later times, which included two paper mills, a wool mill, two corn mills and a brewery. To see a paper mill building, take the right turning from the main road, shortly before reaching the shop. It has recently been renovated and is in use by an electronics firm (1991). Go back towards the pub and turn up on the right behind it. In E.Thomas' yard is an old building where saltpetre was refined for use at the Kennall Gunpowder Works; later it became a guttapercha rubber refinery, owned by ICI. Guttapercha was used in the production of Bickford's safety fuse, which made the use of gunpowder much less hazardous. Just to the left is one of the corn mills. The overshot waterwheel is used for generating; it is a replacement, removed in recent years from a farm in east Cornwall. Go up the road signed "The Mill House" and round behind the house to see the millstream.

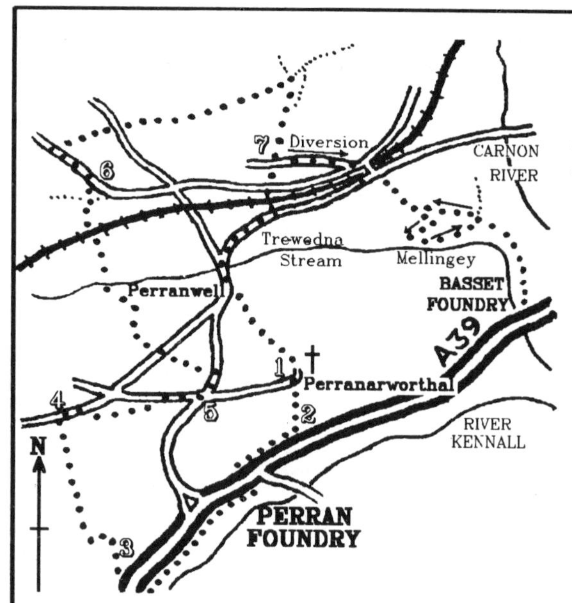

WALK 10

PERRANWELL AND THE PERRAN FOUNDRY

Walks of about two, four-and-a-half and six miles

In 1870 the Rev. Francis Kilvert spent nearly three weeks on holiday in Cornwall. His base was Tullimaar (*), a mansion just east of Perranarworthal Church, and in his diary he recorded what he could see from his window on the first morning: "... the brown sands, mud and shrunk stream of Restronguet, the rich sloping oak woods dark and impervious, rising from the river bed opposite. Down the river beyond the woods may be seen the back of a rounded hill, and up the river the glint of white buildings on the river side, the white walls and chimneys of an iron foundry." This walk takes you to that foundry, one of the most important surviving groups of industrial buildings in Cornwall, already nearly a century old when Kilvert saw it, and also (if you do the full six miles) to another smaller foundry which was still working till very recently. The route includes an old church, a holy well, and attractive countryside - partly woodland and partly a ridgeway track with long views. Unlike any other walk in this book, this one includes over half a mile on a very busy main road, but there is a pavement all the way, and it runs through a valley which is full of historical interest and would be beautiful but for the traffic. ("... the beautiful valley," wrote Kilvert, "seen at its best in the soft golden afternoon sunshine, the white cluster of houses at Devoran down the reach of yellow sand, and above, the grey mansion of Goon Vrea in its woods, the blue hills, tall foundry chimneys and white cottages by the creek shore beneath the woods and hills seen through the soft haze of curling smoke." A pity that the smoke comes from car exhausts now.) The rest of the walk is mostly on minor roads and well-made tracks. There is one very steep and rather muddy climb, but it is mercifully short, and another section of path, beside a stream and through fields, may also be wet. There are pubs, well known locally for good food, at Perranwell (the Royal Oak) and Perranwharf (the Norway Inn), and shops in Perranwell and Perranarworthal.

TULLIMAAR

Although not visible from the walk route (it stands in private grounds among the trees above the main road, east of Perranarworthal Church), this house deserves mention because of its interesting history. It was built about 1828 by Benjamin Sampson, whose wealth derived both from the gunpowder works at Cosawes (Walk 9) and from the Perran Foundry. As I have mentioned, the house features in Kilvert's diary; and in our own century another guest there was General Eisenhower. It is said that an attempt on his life was made by an American soldier while he was at Tullimaar in 1944. It is now the home of the Cornish-born, Nobel-Prize-winning novelist, Sir William Golding, who has kindly supplied me with the following list of interesting people who have lived at Tullimaar. The last one, who owned the house from 1957-73, was a descendant of Napoleon.

A Mrs Hearle-Cock. She transferred an Italianate villa to the grounds of Tullimaar from the Isle of Wight but was in the end forbidden by the council to erect it. She died through being stung by a hornet.

B An illegitimate granddaughter of George III, who was, said the locals with some awe, "buried at royal expense."

C A daughter of David Livingstone.

D Prince and Princess Ghika-Comenesti.

E Princess Bibesco, well thought-on in France as a novelist and "ornament of High Society".

The walk starts at Perranarworthal Church. To drive there from Truro, take the A39 Falmouth road. After about six miles, shortly after the Norway Inn, take the right turning signposted to Perranwell. At the following crossroads, turn right again, following the sign to the church. The church is at the end of this road, and there is a car park at the corner on the left just before you reach it. The Vicar is happy that walkers should use it, providing they avoid times of Sunday services. Bear in mind, too, that if there's a wedding or christening in the church while you're parking, you could get boxed in. There is also some room to park by the road just past the church, but please be careful not to impede farm vehicles.

PERRANARWORTHAL CHURCH

Piran, an Irish saint who is supposed to have floated to Cornwall on a millstone, gave his name to Perranporth, Perranzabuloe and Perranuthnoe, and here his name is linked to that of the ancient manor of Arworthal (meaning "beside the marsh, creek or estuary"). The church dates from Norman times: above the south door, behind glass on the inside of the church, is a Norman tympanum (defined in my dictionary as "a space between a lintel and an arch over it") depicting the Lamb and Cross. The tower was built about 1450. Most of what we see now, however, is the work of Victorian "restorers".

1 Before setting off, you may care to look round the church (*). It is usually kept locked, but a small notice by the main door explains how you can get a key. To start the walk, return along the road you came by for a few yards, past the entrance to a nursery, and go down the footpath signposted to Perran Wharf, which starts on the left via a turnstile. After a short distance there is a side-path on the left, signposted to St Piran's Well. The well is only a few yards away, and worth a look. Any actual connection with St Piran is highly dubious, but "the water is said to contain considerable amounts of iron salts and to have 'general medicinal qualities'."(HW) Francis Kilvert visited it on 6 August 1870, and in his diary wrote a beautiful description, adding, "It is called St Katharine's Well, or the Holy Well." (KCD) J.Meyrick says this is probably not the well from which Perranwell is named, although the site of that is not certain (HWC). Return to the main path, now a metalled drive, and descend to the main road. As you reach it, notice the large limekilns (*) on the right, now serving as stores for the Norway Inn (*). Elisabeth Rowlands mentions that there was "a little arm of the river which gave access to the lime-kilns" until the new part of the turnpike road was built (FRV).

2 Turn right. You are now close to Perranwharf (*) and the even more important later development, Perran Foundry (*). Keep on the right-hand side till you have passed the left turning (Carclew Road). The buildings on

LIMEKILNS

The remains of limekilns are common in Cornwall - a reflection of the high acidity-level of the soil. There were far more on the south coast than the north, mainly because sand containing lime-rich shell fragments was more readily available on the north coast than limestone, most of which came to Cornwall by boat from Plymouth. Kilvert, returning at 3 a.m. from one of the many exhausting expeditions the Hockin family took him on, was still sufficiently awake to notice when they reached Perran Wharf that "A sailing lighter had come up the creek at high tide with a load of limestone, and was lying at the quay waiting to unload and go down again with the next high tide."(KCD) The memories of an elderly resident at Calenick (see Walk 12) are relevant here: "The lime used to come up the river in boats - brown rocks, it was..... They set fire to them somehow in the kiln, and poured water, and then - oh my dear life! - the smoke used to come up and the lime would be white as snow, like dust, and the farmers would come and collect it for their fields." (Quoted in *Calenick Village, A Case Study,* a Project Pack published by the Truro Research Project in 1988.) The way "they set fire to them" was in fact by feeding into the kiln from above alternate layers of coal and limestone and then lighting a coal or wood fire underneath; finally the burnt lime was hydrated or slaked, thus making it suitable for agricultural or building use. The kilns were usually built into the sides of hills or low cliffs so that access from above was easy: see Walk 11 (Point Quay area) for a good example of this. After the middle of the 19th century, limekilns gradually fell out of use, largely because burnt lime was superseded as a fertiliser by crushed limestone brought in by the railways.

THE NORWAY INN

The Norway Inn is usually said to have got its name from the Norwegian vessels which once brought loads of timber to Perran Wharf, largely for use in the mines. A great deal was used underground - for ladders and lining shafts, for example, though not normally for pit-props since these were not usually necessary; the pump-rods and in the early days even the beams for the huge steam-engines were wooden. J.Meyrick in HWC states, however, that the Inn "takes its name from the old family of that name at Flushing." It dates from about 1830, the time when the main Falmouth to Truro road was re-routed to cross the Carnon River on an embankment just above Devoran; the bridge about half a mile further upstream carried the original turnpike, which passed through Perranwell and Calenick. In the days of the Falmouth Packets, the Norway was the first point at which horses were changed by the Falmouth mail coach on its way to London.

PERRANWHARF

In 1769, George Croker Fox, a member of the Quaker family which was already deeply involved in Cornish industry (and which has also bequeathed to Cornwall a legacy of beautiful gardens), bought the lease of what was then a large area of waste land in the lower Kennall valley. He then proceeded to develop it into a port to serve the Gwennap mines, creating jetties, quays, timber ponds and warehouses. For many years the project was highly successful, but the eventual demise of Perranwharf was ensured by the development of Devoran when the railway came, and by the silting-up of Restronguet Creek.

your right include the former Wharf Offices and the Foundry's Counting House, "where the men queued for their pay," says Elisabeth Rowlands, who also suggests that behind the building were stables "where some at least of the twenty four horses needed for hauling heavy castings up the hill in the early days may have been stabled." Cross the main road when the traffic allows, to the Foundry's two entrances. Even if you have to view it from the road, you can get a fair impression of the extent of the buildings (but of course I am writing this before any of Devington's proposed development of the site has taken place). The famous cast-iron lintels bearing the name of the foundry and dated 1791 are over the entrances to the forge building. Continue along the the road. Notice the old building at the bottom of Cove Hill (the road on the right, where the general store and post office is): this was Manor Mill, a corn and grist mill which had two waterwheels served by a leat taken from the Kennall River a little downstream from where the railway viaduct now is. (See Walk 9.) The date of the mill is uncertain, but there are records of its existence in 1692. Ivy Edwards refers to it as "Little Mill" in FRV. Devington's original plans for the Foundry site would have entailed demolition of the Manor Mill to make way for a roundabout, but Mr Lawrence Butler of Devington's tells me that the roundabout is now likely to be sited further north. On the opposite side of Cove Hill from the mill is Tredrea, the house built about 1740 as their own home by the Fox

Directions continue on page 102.

THE PERRAN FOUNDRY (Colour picture 21)

Perran Foundry was built on part of the site of Perranwharf by Fox's two sons, George Croker Junior and Robert Were. It was not Cornwall's first large engine-factory (that was built by John Harvey at Hayle in 1779), but it followed close behind, in 1791, and in this year of its 200th birthday it remains one of the most interesting and impressive monuments to the heyday of Cornish industry, despite recent neglect and demolition threats. The most interesting account of the history of Perran Foundry that I have come across is Elisabeth Rowlands' in FRV; there is also a good brief account in IAC(2), which includes a list of some of the most important engines built at the Foundry. For another good source of information, seek out HAF, Vol.1. T.H.Bradley's article concentrates on the water-power at the foundry, but the plan on pages 40-1 gives a clearer picture of the extent and layout of the works than any words could. A second leat was taken from the Kennall River close to the Manor Mill leat but on the south side, and on its way down to the foundry this was joined by the stream from the old gunpowder works at Cosawes (Walk 9) and another stream at Treluswell. It was then sufficient to run at least five waterwheels at the foundry. Business flourished: by 1860 the works covered 6 acres, had 400 employees and was exporting steam engines all over the world as well as supplying local industry. One of Robert Were Fox's sons, Barclay, kept a journal, and some of the entries convey well the atmosphere of the foundry in its great days, such as this one from 1840: "Arrived at Perran just in time to see the casting of the great bob - 14 tons. A most superb sight; the impetuous lava stream, the eager anxiety of the men regulating the speed and direction of the dazzling flood, and the blood-vessel-bursting excitement of Richard Cloke was altogether a scene quite cyclopean." This bob or beam was probably for the famous 85" "Taylor's Engine", installed at United Mines. The engines for export were loaded on to flat-bottomed barges and transferred to sea-going vessels at a quay near the Pandora Inn which the Foxes had acquired, or further down-river. According to IAC(2), "There is some evidence that boilers were even floated down the river." For more information about the engines and other equipment made at the foundry, see BE, CBE and the recent reprint of the foundry's catalogue of about 1870 (see Walk 3, the note on Twelveheads). The foundry had its own gasworks to provide lighting, and I have heard the claim made that the cottages at Foundry Terrace (now called Glenside), on the hill above, were the first houses in the world to be lit by "mains" gas. The slump in the mining industry during the 1870s hit Perran Foundry badly, and it closed in 1879. As described by Ivy Edwards in FRV and by T.H.Bradley in HAF Part 3, the buildings were later adapted for the handling of textiles and the milling and storage of grains and animal foods; another waterwheel was added. More recently the old foundry has belonged to the Bibby group, who used it mainly as a store. In 1988 Devington Ltd. put forward plans to convert the buildings without destroying their original character, into a 4-star hotel-cum-restaurant at the western end of the site, residential apartments and cottages at the eastern end, and a "Heritage Centre" in the middle, including a museum and facilities for exhibitions, concerts, presentation of plays and public meetings. Devington's concern for conservation and historical accuracy was illustrated in January 1990, when the Managing Director, Mr Lawrence Butler, appealed for information about the original external appearance of the gasworks , and the press reported his desire to protect bat colonies in the old buildings. In August 1990 the Carrick Planning Subcommittee approved Devington's scheme in principle, but with several conditions, one of which required that before building work starts time should be allowed for the Cornwall Archaeological Unit to carry out a survey of the site. Mr Tony Rowland's Newsletter to the Friends of Perran Foundry, February 1991, reported that during October and November, "Ten trial trenches were dug in selected areas to investigate the buried deposits on various parts of the site. Some interesting discoveries were made. In the smiths' shop a system of underfloor passages was found which carried draught from a fan engine to the individual smiths' hearths. The hearths themselves have not survived. In the hammer mill the wheelpit of the water wheel which powered the trip hammers was excavated to a depth of two metres. The loadings and mounting bolts for the trip hammer remained in situ on one side. A particularly exciting discovery was part of the bed of a reverberatory furnace which was discovered in the loam moulding shop. It is likely that the remainder of the furnace lies beneath the concrete. This is thought to be the only surviving mid-19th century air furnace known in this country." (For reverberatory furnaces, see the note on Newham smelting house, Walk 12.) At the time of writing (April 1991), objections by English Heritage to the proposed scale of new

The main entrance to the forge building at Perran Foundry (1989). On the right is the Machines and Fitting Shop.

residential development have led Devington's to consider abandoning the plan for a hotel so that more residential accommodation can be provided within the existing buildings. Clearly, much still remains to be decided.

The above sketch, which I have included with the kind permission of Mr Lawrence Butler of Devington's, is based on an artist's impression of the Foundry as it will look if the current plans are carried out. Compare the old engraving, which views the buildings from the same angle.

family, founders of Perranwharf and the Foundry. The Manor Mill leat also once powered a waterwheel for water pumping at Tredrea. (In our century Tredrea became a hotel, and is now divided into flats.) The next turning on the right, which joins Cove Hill higher up, is the old turnpike road to Truro, as mentioned in the note on the Norway Inn. Soon after this, also on the right, is Goonvrea, another house built by the Foxes; this too became a hotel. Recently it suffered a bad fire. The Kennall River is on your left; the water-meadows beside it and Devichoys Wood above ("burnt wood": see the note on Burnthouse Wood, Walk 9) are now under the protection of the Cornwall Trust for Nature Conservation. Round about now you need to cross back to the right side of the main road.

3 Before long you will reach a large layby where farm produce is usually on sale. At the far end of this, opposite the bus stop, turn right up the public footpath to Perrandowns. After the entrance to Polpentre it becomes a steep, narrow path. At the top, turn right on a wider track. Keep to this as it curves left and right, and go straight on where a metalled drive on the right leads to a bungalow. (The view here includes Perranwell to the left, with the railway line this side of it; Perranarworthal Church further right with Carnon Downs on the hill above; Devoran further right again.) Notice the pump on the left.

4 At the road turn right, passing the lodge at the entrance to Goonvrea; after about fifty yards take the track on the right, and at the road turn right again.

5 Turn left on to St Piran's Hill at the crossroads. Soon on the left there is a small side-road (Treworthal Road). The walk continues along the footpath on the left immediately after that - but if you are ready for refreshments you may prefer to continue up the road into Perranwell. (On the other hand, you might care to postpone this, because the route passes through Perranwell later.) From Perranwell you could shorten the walk to a total of about two

The Perran Foundry. This engraving was probably made soon after the Norway Inn was built, in the 1830s. (Courtesy R.I.C.)

miles by returning direct to the church, following the directions from near the end of point 7; otherwise, return to the path mentioned above, by Treworthal Road. After a granite stile, cross the road and continue along the path opposite, signposted Rissick. At the junction, bear right (not sharp right), following the sign to Chyvogue House. Bear left, ignoring the stile in the fence ahead, and now you pass the entrance to Chyvogue House (*) and The Old Mill. Turn right beside the building, over a footbridge and along by the Trewedna Stream, which served this mill. (It continues through Perranwell to Mellingey Creek, where it provided power for a smelting works and Basset Foundry: some details are given later.) Cross the stile and then bear slightly right, away from the stream, crossing the field to a high stone stile topped by a metal rail. Next, bear left, keeping wall and hedge on your left, to another stone stile, and pass under the bridge carrying the Falmouth-Truro branch line (1863). Soon another track cuts across; here, cross the stile straight ahead, walk by the hedge on the right and go through the gate to the road.

CHYVOGUE

During Elizabethan times tin was mined in the Perrandowns area, just south of here, and the stamps were at Chyvogue, which means "the place of the furnace" (compare Vogue, on the edge of St Day). The 1908 O.S. map shows a "Woollen Factory" here - it manufactured mainly blankets - and by 1900 there was also a saw-mill.

6 Turn left, and after about a quarter of a mile, just past Hawthorn Farm, turn right past a bungalow's entrance, taking the track which leads off uphill on the right. At the road, carry straight on along this ridgeway which later gives you good views south. Still continue when the track narrows to a (probably muddy) path, and as you approach a farm on the right, watch for a high stile on that side. Cross this and walk to the right side of the farmhouse, where there is another stile; pass along the house-side, then by the hedge till you come to a stile to the main track on your left. Cross on to this and turn right. Now you have good views over Devoran and Restronguet Creek.

7 At the road, you have a choice: (a) Turn left for an interesting diversion of under two miles, following the directions below, headed Mellingey Diversion ; or (b) Take the direct route back to the church, as follows: Cross the road and continue down the footpath, signposted to Perranwell. At the next road turn left and then immediately right, through a kissing-gate to cross the railway line (with due care!). Turn right at the road - watch for fast traffic here. After the chapel, bear left and take the public footpath to the church on the left just before the Post Office. (The Royal Oak is just a little beyond the Post Office, on the right.) The path to the church, which crosses two stone cattle-grids, is about half a mile long.

MELLINGEY DIVERSION

Turn left on the road, as stated at the start of point 7, and at the T-junction turn left; soon afterwards turn right, crossing the railway bridge, and at the following T-junction take the path opposite. Fork right where the paths divide and continue along a narrow path among trees. At the house with a granite wall, turn right on to a path between hedges, rather overgrown at first. At the point where this becomes too overgrown to continue comfortably, turn sharp left beside the stream flowing through what was once Mellingey (mill) Creek (*); the area appears on the maps now as Tarrandean. This brings you past The Stables to the main track. Here it's worth making a diversion within the diversion by turning right and continuing down almost to the main (A39) road. This takes you alongside the part of the Bissoe Valley where tin-streaming was still being carried out by Hydraulic Tin till about ten years ago, and finally to the engineering works generally known as Visick's, which began life as Basset Foundry (*). In 1987 it was bought by the King Harry Steam Ferry Company, and over the next couple of years reportedly had a healthy order book for the marine parts it manufactured, but in July 1990 *The West Briton* announced unofficially that the firm was expected to close at the end of August. From here, return by the same route as far as The Stables, and then continue along the main track, bearing slightly left, which returns you to the road by the railway bridge. Now turn left and walk with care along this fairly busy road. After about half a mile you reach Perranwell chapel; from there follow the directions in the last four lines of point 7.

MELLINGEY CREEK

It is hard now to believe that until at least the end of the 18th century Mellingey Creek was navigable, and that timber and mining supplies could be landed. By about 1650, a blowing house for smelting tin was built here (close to where the path turns sharp left); about 1690 it was enlarged, and in 1774 was described as having five furnaces, two stamping mills and a house with eight stables. Before long, though, the Bissoe Valley tin-streaming had completely cut off Mellingey Creek to boats, and the blowing house closed, to be converted in 1812 into an arsenic works - in fact, according to D.B.Barton, this marked "the first beginnings of industrial arsenic production in Britain". In 1840 it began dealing with heavily contaminated ores, and at once local people started complaining of bad smells and the poisoning of bees and even livestock; the owner was brought to court in 1851, lost the case, and by 1856 had closed down the works. (See PV, page 41.) Despite one attempt to revive it (1866-70), it became derelict, and now it is difficult to find any trace of its existence.

THE BASSET FOUNDRY

This enterprise presumably took its name from the Bassets of Tehidy, who owned land in these parts: for example, Tullimaar was built on land leased from them. The Basset Foundry began in 1858; after a period of prosperity it succumbed, like its larger neighbour at Perran, to the problems created by the mining depression, and in 1876 was converted into the Cornwall & Devon Chemical Manure and Bone Works. The largest building was the bone mill, and its walls are still visible. This new enterprise survived only six years, and the buildings lay derelict till 1895 when Walter Visick, a former Perran Foundry employee, took out a 60-year lease and risked making large investments in a new engineering works at a time of general decline in Cornish industry. He rebuilt the two existing waterwheels on the west side, and made a dam on the east side to control the flow of the Trewedna Stream and provide power for another waterwheel, built in 1905. The remains of this can still be seen from the footpath. By manufacturing a wide range of smaller items like lamp-posts, manhole covers and Cornish ranges, the new factory prospered. (For most of the information in the last two notes, I am indebted to T.H.Bradley's article in HAF, Part 2. For a very detailed account of the history of the Foundry, see Part 5 in the same series.)

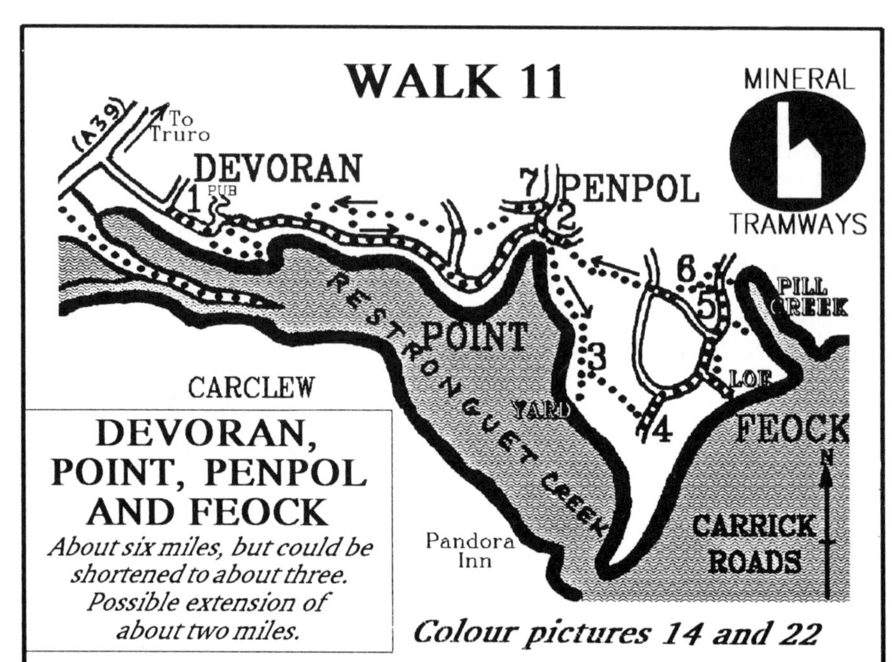

Even if old industries are the most boring topic in the world for you, you will enjoy this walk for its scenic beauty; but it also holds a wealth of interest for the industrial archaeologist. After looking at the port that handled most of the traffic from the mineral railway, we follow the course of that railway along the side of Restronguet Creek - itself the scene of at least four ventures in tin streaming and underwater tin mining. At Penpol, we take the story of the mining industry a little further by turning our attention to the smelting of the ores - a topic treated more fully in Walk 12. All this is covered in the three-mile walk; the six-mile version perhaps doesn't add greatly to the theme of Cornish industry, but is delightful walking and provides panoramic views, including one that takes in much of the territory covered by this book. An extra stroll of two miles or less is suggested as an interesting appendix. The main walk is mostly on lanes and country roads, but there are several short stretches of path which are likely to be muddy; advice is given on how to avoid the worst of these if you prefer. Devoran has a pub and several shops; there is also a shop at Feock.

To drive to Devoran from Truro, take the A39 south towards Falmouth. After about five miles you reach the main turning to Devoran on the left, but continue a little further, just past the Bissoe turning (right). Take the next turning left, and where this road turns left into the village, go straight on for a few yards, into Quay Road. You should find parking space here, either beside the road on the right, or in a space on the left. (Please note: these directions were written before the completion of the Carnon Downs bypass, which will presumably end at a roundabout at the point where you turn into Devoran.)

1 Walk along Quay Road, past the village hall. You are now going along the course of the main Redruth and Chasewater Railway line serving Devoran Quay, and on the far side of the village hall ran the branch which continued to Point. The hall building was originally the railway's workshops, and Old Quay House, a few yards further, was the office buildings. (Notice the picture of Spitfire on the house name-plate: see the note about the railway in Walk 3.) Intriguingly, several granite "setts" or sleeper blocks (easily recognisable by the pair of bolt-holes in each) have been used in the building, not only of the garden wall of Old Quay House, but also of the house itself and of the village hall; the only explanation for this that I can think of is that both buildings were erected at the time when heavy-duty rails were being laid to bear the weight of the new locomotives (about 1854), and that the original setts were replaced at the same time. Several other setts are lying beside the road, one or two with much of the original metal plate still *in situ.* On the right nearby, the parking-space in front of the bungalow called Smelter's Rest (referring to another of the engines) has an arrangement of small granite blocks that looks like the junction of a siding, but whether this is a genuine relic I don't know. The last house on the left, recently converted, was a sail loft. Just past Quay House, where the road turns left take the narrow footpath bearing right, on to Devoran Quay (*). Walk to the far end, where a fine job has been done recently by the Devoran Quay Preservation Society in restoring parts of the quay to something close to their original form. Follow the foreshore as it curves round a small inlet (several more

Devoran Quay in 1990, showing some of the reconstruction work recently carried out. On the right can be seen some of the old storage hutches.

DEVORAN QUAY

On your right when you first walk on to it are the upper parts of what was once a complex system of wharves and docks, now gardens and bungalows. Downriver, only one modern building has encroached on the quay area, and the ruins survive of at least eight of the old "hutches", where copper ore was stored ready for shipment to South Wales. According to the 1908 O.S. map, reproduced below, there were once twelve of them, plus a larger building beyond. The railway line ran on a wooden structure behind them, level with the tops of the walls (then about 10-12 feet high), so that the ore could be tipped in. It was transferred to the ships by barrow. On the site of the modern bungalow was the engine-shed; nearby were several stables, because right up to the time of the railway's closure in 1915 horses were used, not only on the extension to Point, but also to pull wagons along the numerous sidings at Devoran. The quay itself was wooden, because stone walls were hard to build on the shifting mud; wood faggots were used to bind the mud, and then sixteen-feet-long timber piles were driven in. A diary entry from 1838 reads: "Expense of 216 feet of wharf frontage: £243-0-6." Several granite mooring bollards have survived. At the same time as the wharf was built, a reservoir was dug with sluice-gates so that water could be released periodically to flush out silt. The coming of the railway and the docks led to a growth in Devoran's population from 205 in 1841 to 1500 in 1871; the two attractive long terraces of stone-fronted houses were built about 1850. After about 1870 the decline of the Gwennap copper industry, combined with the ever-worsening problem of the silt, spelt trouble for Devoran Quay. In 1876 the County Adit (see Walk 3) became blocked near its mouth at Twelveheads; the following winter was very wet, and when the pent-up waters in the mines finally broke free so much silt was deposited down-river that from then on ships had to discharge much of their cargo at Point before continuing to Devoran. The last ship delivered coal at Devoran in 1916. For further details, including several interesting old maps, plans and photographs, see DDCV.

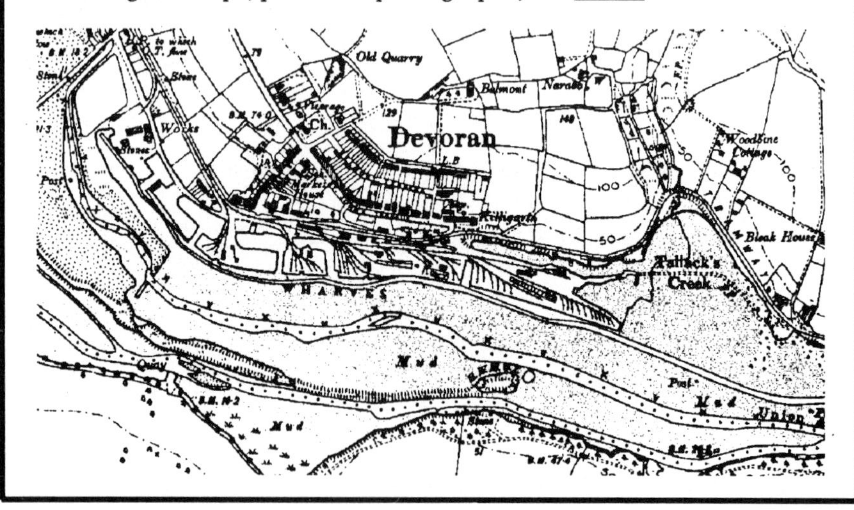

sleeper blocks round here) and then beside a larger one, Narabo Creek. Now the path goes to the left of a quite large ruined building, perhaps a railway warehouse, which is shown on the 1908 map, and later to the right of two smaller ones, perhaps stables. Turn right on the gravelled drive, right again at the road, and right a third time (unless you're ready to call at the Old Quay Inn now) on to the Old Tram Road, which follows the course of the railway to Point. After a quarter of a mile or less, the road curves round Tallack's Creek. At the end of this part, just beyond the letter box fixed to a telegraph pole, go down on the right to look at the remains of the engine house of the Carnon Stream Mine (*). Return to the road and continue. The

THE CARNON STREAM MINE

See Walk 3 for information about alluvial tin in the Carnon Valley. From the late 18th century until 1812, a big area of the valley bottom, from Carnon Gate (where the old main road from Perranwell ran to Truro) to Tallack's Creek, was sealed off by embankments, with a dam at the seaward end. Inside this enclosure tin streaming was carried out; ancient tools made of wood and antler were found, plus some gold: a nugget 5.5cms long is displayed in the County Museum, Truro. George Henwood, lecturing in 1853, recalled the scene here: "a machine in a desert of red sand heaped into vast piles and hollows, the only herbage being a few tufts of sea daisy, while here and there in the trenches might be seen tinners working knee deep in water and a few squalid, half-clad boys wheeling the tin ore to the stream head in barrows." In 1812, the dam was swept away during a storm, and now almost the only visible remains of that huge enterprise, which yielded profits of about £5,000, are the low-tide footpaths near the Carclew side and across Tallack's Creek, which follow the lines of embankments. Plenty of tin remained, and by 1818 plans were afoot to sink a shaft in the middle of the creek just below where the tin streaming had ceased, and to erect a powerful steam engine and water pump on the shore. These were complete by 1824. In 1828 the railway company officially complained that the new mine-workings were impeding shipping, and the mine seems to have closed soon after that, but during its short lifetime it made a profit of £28,000. The remaining wall of the engine house is "one of the oldest industrial relics surviving in Cornwall" according to MSC, but Kenneth Brown points out that we don't know that it dates from 1824 as there were other engines.

old pump on the right a little later is a reminder that mains water came to the houses near here for the first time only recently; they all have their own wells. The unspoilt woods and farmland on the opposite side of the creek are parts of the Carclew (*) estate. After about another half-mile, on the left just before Gulls Haven bungalow, is a well preserved limekiln. This was almost completely hidden by vegetation when I wrote the original *Carn Marth;* the reason for its emergence is explained in the note about Daniell's Point. Gulls Haven is roughly on the site once occupied by the surface buildings of the Restronguet Creek Tin Works (*). The next turning left is to Point Green - worth a look as one of Cornwall's few village greens, and a very attractive

CARCLEW

The great house of Carclew was built in 1728 for Samuel Kempe, a gentleman from Penryn who had married into the Bonython family, owners of Carclew Barton. In 1749 it was bought, together with its deer park, gardens and plantations covering more than a square mile, by William Lemon, who had made a vast fortune, mainly from the copper mines. (His name is perpetuated in Lemon Street and Lemon Quay, Truro, as well as Lemon Hill and the Lemon Arms at Mylor Bridge.) Carclew House was burnt down in 1934, and little remains except part of the Ionic façade. The splendid gardens, famous for their rhododendrons, lily pond and lake, are occasionally opened to the public: for details, see the annual *Gardens of Cornwall Open Guide,* published by the Cornwall Garden Society. For more about William Lemon and Carclew, see Joan Rea's article in HAF Part 5, and the note on Princes House in Walk 12.

THE RESTRONGUET CREEK TIN WORKS

In 1871 a shaft was sunk here to a depth of 90 feet and a cast-iron ventilation shaft was driven down 76 feet to the tin-bearing level in the middle of the creek by fastening barges loaded with 250 tons of stone to the top at high tide. At low water, the top of the iron shaft is still visible. ("Did you know," Mr Anthony Cartwright wrote in a recent letter to me, "that air bubbles from the old ventilation shaft still rise to the surface of the creek like soda-water?")During the next eight years a complex pattern of "levels" was mined between here and the old Carnon Stream Mine. An engine for pumping was housed close to the limekiln, but apparently drainage presented few problems even though there was 14 feet of water above the workings at high tide. For the full story, see Volume 2 of ECMH. This was the last mining venture on (or under) Restronguet Creek, but as recently as the early 1980s an international company caused much local controversy by putting forward a scheme to dredge the creek bed for the wealth of minerals that still remains. Falling tin prices put paid to that, as to so many earlier and later enterprises.

one, complete with an old pump. Once the Green had a pub, the Bell Inn. Continuing along the creekside road, you immediately reach what was once known as Daniell's Point (*), with its long old building, the near end of which was apparently a smithy in the days of the railway. During 1990 it has been converted into two luxury houses. Opposite is a brick-built pair of houses - a quite unusual sight in these parts. As my copy of the 1857 painting shows, there was a tall stack here, part of the Penpoll smelting works (*), and when this was demolished the bricks were used to build the houses. Continue round into Penpol (or Penpoll) Creek. Soon after Black Lane, on the left (perhaps so named because of the smoke from all the industrial chimneys once here: the old painting shows seventeen!), you reach the site of the main smelting works buildings, now occupied by Polmarion. You may still be able to see relics of the concrete floors or yard, and of flues in the wall behind. On the right here was another wharf, and close to the wall you may be able to make out what could be a small buddle (*). Go on for

DANIELL'S POINT

The Daniell family (see Walk 12) built a quay here before 1800, capable then of taking ships over 160 tons. Apart from a probable short extension to the Penpoll Smelting Works, the railway line ended at this quay. Several small granite setts are still visible. (Can you find them?) Now known as Point Quay, it was purchased as a public amenity in 1989 by Feock Parish Council with the aid of £33,000 raised locally through the Point Quay Association. At the same time the nearby orchard was also bought, and the limekiln there has been brought to light by the voluntary effort of local people. In May 1991 they were hard at work on the quay itself, erecting seats and car-barriers. The name, "Regatta Cottage", alludes to the Point and Penpol Regatta, one of the leading annual events in the local yachting calendar and justly famous for its excellent teas.

THE PENPOLL SMELTING WORKS

In 1817, Sir William Lemon, grandson of the William Lemon who had Princes House built (Walk 12), leased land on the western shore of Penpol Creek, roughly opposite the site of the former boatyard, for the building of a wharf to be named Lemon Quay. By 1827 a lead smelting works had been built beside the new quay. By 1880 the works was owned by the London-based Penpoll Tin Smelting Company, who had converted the original buildings for tin smelting and set up a new lead smelting plant closer to Point. Flues were built up to tall stacks on the higher land behind both smelting houses. Closure came in 1921.

Point and Penpol in their industrial heyday - compare the drawing on the title page. This sketch is based on a watercolour painted in 1857.

> ***BUDDLE***
> Here is C.C.James's definition of "buddles" in HPG: "Pits, 7 feet long and 3 feet wide and 2.5 feet deep, dug near a stamping mill. Stamped tin is curiously washed from its impurities by water constantly running through the buddles, while a boy is standing in it working with a shovel and also with his feet." Circular buddles were a later introduction: see PV, page 11.

another couple of hundred yards, until you come to stepping stones on the right - perhaps submerged. In their place was once a tide mill used to power bone-crushing machinery; beyond it was Bone Mill Pond. The bone mill was built in 1829, presumably mainly to supply bonemeal as a fertiliser.

2 Now the time for a choice has come: either return directly to Devoran or continue to Feock. For the former, go to the bridge at the head of Penpol Creek and on past the chapel to a left turning; then follow the directions from point 7. To walk to Feock (and it's very worthwhile), cross the stepping stones if the water is low enough; if not, walk to the head of the creek and take the track on the right beside the foreshore. (At exceptionally high tides you may have to use the road above, through the estate.) The foreshore along here has a heavy scattering of clinker, presumably a relic of the Penpol smelting works. Follow track or foreshore (or road) round to the site of Penpol Boatyard, and then either take the lane straight ahead, marked "Unsuitable for heavy goods vehicles", or at low tide continue along the foreshore, if you don't mind picking your way over, under or around the various mooring ropes and piles of nautical paraphernalia. The boatyard had been idle for some months before the gales early in 1990 damaged some of the buildings, all of which were then removed. At the time of writing no planning application for development of the site had been submitted. During the winter for many years dozens of small craft have been laid up in this part of Penpol Creek; when we first came to live here, nearly ten years ago, two concrete barges provided extra shelter; later these were towed away and moored in King Harry Reach, and three rusty hulks replaced them. Following a protest campaign led by many local residents as these vessels became more and more decrepit, two of them were dismantled and removed, and as I write the third one is very gradually being cut into small lumps. Still there (but for how much longer?) are the disintegrating remains of a motor torpedo boat; it is hardly believable now, from this evidence, that MTBs were the fastest vessels in service during World War 2.

3 The foreshore route will bring you to the small headland called Carnon Yard (*); if you are using the lane above, bear right where it forks, after nearly half a mile. From Carnon Yard return the same way, and on re-joining the original lane, turn right towards Harcourt (spelt "Harket" on some old maps, and probably meaning "beside or facing the rock"). At the bungalow called Tweseldown, go straight on ahead to a narrow path and over the stile. (Often muddy here!) You will have occasional glimpses of the Pandora Inn across Restronguet Creek: see Walk 3 in *Around the Fal.* After the farm buildings, follow the lane past the houses at Harcourt till you reach the road.

4 Turn left and take the road to the right just past Porthgwidden gatehouse,

CARNON YARD AND THE CARNON MINE

This point is known as Yard because it had a boat-building yard. Sheila Bird's *Around the Waterways of the Fal*, 1988, gives details of some of the locally famous vessels built here by the Ferris family in the 1850s and 60s. Before that, however, the engine house of the Carnon Mine (1835-42) stood here. An island, still visible at low tide, was created out in the creek and a shaft twelve feet in diameter was sunk into this "by the laborious expedient of covering the cylinder top and shovelling sufficient silt on to it that the weight - as much as a hundred tons - forced it down in successive stages." (TMSC) A small pumping-engine was then erected by the shaft. By 1838 the mine was employing 212 people, but this was a costly operation, and tin prices fell, so the mine lost about £16,000.

into Feock. Porthgwidden ("white harbour" or "white gate") is an old house whose estates once extended as far as Restonguet Point; it is now, in Mrs Satchwell's words, "tastefully converted into flats and maisonettes". Soon you come to a right turning signposted Loe (Cornish *loch*, "pool") Beach, a pleasant spot with a fine view of Carrick Roads. The main walk route carries on along the road to the church, but if you decide to go down to the beach, you can avoid part of the steep walk back by taking the path to the right, marked Feock, just before a wooden garage. At first keep close to the wall on the left, then head for the stumpy spire of Feock church (*). There is a telephone box at the point where you re-join the road. Turn right, and after looking at the church continue along the road past the post-office-cum-shop and the lych gate.

FEOCK CHURCH AND VILLAGE

St Feoca's church is said to have been where the last sermon in the Cornish language was preached. The church itself was so heavily "restored" in 1874 that hardly anything old remains, but the detached tower dates from the 13th century. There is also a Norman font made of "Cataclewse stone", quarried from Cataclews Point near Harlyn Bay (see *Around Padstow*, Walk 2), and in the south porch is a set of stocks. In the churchyard is a Celtic cross, with a crowned figure of Christ on one side and a decorative Gothic cross on the other. Nothing at all is known of "St Feoca"; in her history of the village, *Introducing Feock* (obtainable at the village shop), S.M.Satchwell suggests that the word "Feock" may derive from *feage* or *vegue*, "a lofty local place". She points out that the upper part of the village is called "La Feock"; *La* is a version of *lan*, "church-site or hermitage", and the name is pronounced "La *vaig*" (Padel). There is a well in La Feock Lane, and Mrs Satchwell suggests that an unnamed monk may have set up his hermitage there and become known as "the holy man on the hill" or Saint Feock. The old and modern photographs in *Introducing Feock* suggest that the appearance of the older part of the village has changed very little over the past century, but one considerable change did occur when the village school, near the church, closed in 1983; the number of pupils had fallen from a maximum of 104 in the days when it was an all-age school, to just 13.

5 After the right and left bends, take the tarmacked footpath on the right, beside the entrance to the Church Hall car park,which brings you down to Pill Creek(*). If the tide is low enough, go down the steps to the foreshore and walk along to the left (but if not, see the note in italics opposite). Near the head of the creek there is a wooden boathouse on the left; go up the

PILL CREEK

Pill Creek (oddly named, since "pill" means creek) was for a time important to the copper mines as a port for shipping ore and importing coal. Look across the creek from the point where the path brings you down. The right-hand house of the attractive pair was a pub, and the ships docked at the quay below it. (See page 53 in HAF Part 5 for a list of the items in William Lemon's Office and Chambers at Pill in 1760; apparently "quite a convivial place", as Joan Rea remarks.) The problem with ports like this one and Roundwood Quay, a little further up-river (see Walk 4 in *Around the Fal),* was the land communications. (A letter of January 1817 reads, ".... such frequent rains for the last month - the roads from the mines to the wharf are so badly cut up, particularly those to Pill, that all the wheel carriages are stopped and the mules are the only conveyance at present.") Canals were considered, but engineers declared them impracticable, and the hills precluded a railway. The arrival of the Redruth and Chasewater at Devoran ensured that Pill Creek would return to peace and quiet.

tarmacked path just beyond this to return to the road. There turn right, and after a short distance turn sharp left on to a concreted lane, signposted to La Feock. Just past the house called Gelvinack (but house names have a habit of changing), take the footpath on the right, again signposted to La Feock. (*If the tide is too high for walking on the foreshore, return up the same path, turn right at the road, and after about 200 yards, at the top of the slope, take the footpath on the left, turning left again where signposted to La Feock, just past Seascape and Landfall.)* Keep by the hedge on the right - a good view down Carrick Roads from here - and go through the (muddy) gateway; now the path weaves left and right beside two houses. After the second one, The Old Grange, notice the pump and well on the left (the well referred to in the note about Feock).

6 Turn right at the road, and at the T-junction cross the stile (concrete steps beside a gate) immediately opposite. Walk straight ahead, keeping the hedge to your left. At and just after the next stile you have a good panoramic view of Penpol Creek and beyond to Restronguet Creek and Devoran, with Carn Marth on the horizon. Continue straight on down the field, emerging via a farm gate on to a lane. Cross the stile opposite, by Trolver farm, and go on in the same direction. After the next stile you walk among modern bungalows and come to a road. At the road, continue downhill into Penpol, passing the chapel on your right.

7 Turn left over the bridge and walk quite steeply uphill past old cottages at first, then new houses. Take the first left turning, a rough track, and follow it round as it curves to the right. This was once a ropewalk - compare Walk 12, near the end of section 3. At the road, turn right, then immediately left on to a muddy track. (If it is too muddy, you could instead walk back down the road towards the creek, passing through Point Green, and taking the path on the right which leads down to the Old Tram Road; it starts beside the last of the row of houses overlooking the green. This brings you back to Devoran.) If you decide to brave the mire, walk along the track behind houses. It dips into a valley at Chycoose Farm and then continues ahead. Still a bit more mud to come, but the view of Restronguet Creek a bit further on will compensate. At the end of the field with a hedge to your left, you could cross the high stile just before a gate and go down to the Tram Road; or go through the gate, keep by the hedge, and turn left down the drive at the next house. Turn right on the creekside road to return to your starting-point.

A POSSIBLE EXTRA

Before you leave Devoran - or perhaps on another day - you may care to do an extra walk of a little under two miles. For this, walk back along the road you originally drove into Devoran by (Greenbank Road). At the start of it, just opposite what used to be the Devoran Bakery on the corner, Carclew Terrace follows the former railway track; until the road was widened at the corner recently, the original crossing-gate was hidden in a hedge there; it is visible in my drawing between the engine and the wagon. One of the two granite gate-posts is still in place, and the other has been set up in a new position, but the correct distance away, so that the restored original gate or a replica could be hung between them. Several sidings - as the picture suggests - went to the quay from the main line, crossing what is now

Miner at Devoran, probably about 1900. The wagon is at or near the bottom of Market Street. In the background is Carn Marth.

Greenbank Road, and if as you walk along that you look left at the first opening you will see a line of setts by the hedge. Turn left at the main road, crossing the Carnon Valley on the embankment and passing the filling station. Before you reach the trees on the far side there is a small path on the left which runs along an embankment (a relic of the tin-streaming days, when the tides had to be kept at bay: see the note on the Carnon Stream Mine), and if you go as far along this as the state of the tide permits you have an interesting view of the various streams (Trewedna, Kennall and Carnon) joining the creek here, and later of the Devoran waterfront, the Carnon Stream Mine engine-house, and on the right the woods of Carclew. If you go as far as the last tiny islet, make sure a rising tide doesn't cut off your retreat!

Devoran Quay at about the same time.

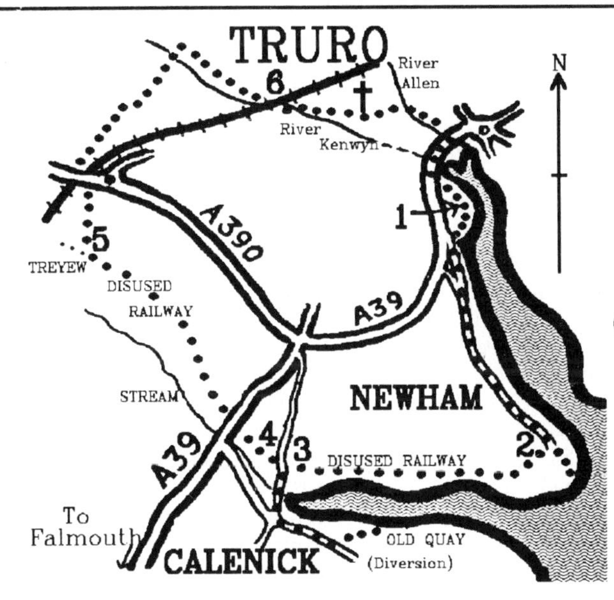

WALK 12

TRURO, NEWHAM AND CALENICK

About four miles, plus a possible diversion of less than a mile.

This is a walk of great contrasts, ranging from city-centre streets to Truro's answer to the Camel Trail. The footpath created from the former Newham Branch Line is of course much shorter than Padstow-to-Wenfordbridge, but it strongly rivals it for beauty, especially if you walk it during the winter months when there are no leaves on the trees to hide Calenick Creek; and in one respect it is better from the pedestrian's viewpoint: cyclists are not permitted to use it. For those interested in industrial history the walk offers a great deal, as the large number of boxed notes implies. The section of the walk within Truro city is very rich in historical detail; in order not to overload this part of the book I have focused mainly on what relates to mining history. It is an easy walk, mostly flat and on well-made tracks, minor roads and streets; the optional diversion at Calenick involves field-paths and therefore possibly mud underfoot. The only pubs, shops and public toilets on the route are in Truro.

Directions are given from and back to the long-stay car park next to Tesco's, beside the main by-pass road (A39, Morlaix Avenue - named after Truro's twin town).

1 Go to the pavement beside the main road; turn right and right again immediately on to the riverside walk, which takes you along Garras Wharf (*). On the top of the hill to your left is Truro School. Continue beside the Truro River with Tesco's car park on your right at first and then along Newham Road on a pavement which was just being completed when we walked this route again for the new book. Newham, in Kea parish, was one of the four manors whose estates covered the area now occupied by Truro, the others being Trehaverne (Kenwyn parish), Moresk and Polwhele (both in St Clement parish). The name "Newham" indicates the Saxon origin of this settlement; following the Conquest the Lords of Newham were, of course, Norman, by name de Pridyas, and they tried to secure borough status for it,

GARRAS WHARF AND TRURO AS A PORT

As you walk along Garras Wharf, just a couple of hundred yards behind you, beyond the main road, is Lemon Quay. If St Day church is a symbol of St Day's decline as a mining town, Lemon Quay forms a parallel in Truro's history as a port: in 1923, after centuries of busy maritime activity, the river there was concreted over and turned into a car park. Of course, motor vehicles were just one factor among many that caused the change: bigger ships, silting and the growth of Falmouth were others. Records as far back as 1160 indicate Truro's importance in the exporting of tin and wool. In Tudor times, ships of 100 tons used Truro, and as the mining industry grew, so the port facilities expanded, with numerous quays and wharfs, often named after the men who had them built to serve their own businesses (Lemon, Enys, Worth, and presumably also Garras, are examples). The climax of shipping activity came in the 19th century, even though by then the silt excluded ships over 30 tons, and the cargoes from larger vessels had to be brought up from Malpas by barge. "In the ten days from 17 March to 26 March 1873," writes David Mudd (*About the City,* Bossiney Books, 1979), "forty-two ships arrived with coal, nitrates, timber, grain and flour." There was also a timber-yard, where rafts of imported timber were left in water to season. Despite the decline, Truro has never quite died as a port: a few cargo vessels (many bringing timber from Scandinavia) have continued to weave their way up the deep-water channels along with the pleasure-boats, and the 1988-9 guide published by the Chamber of Commerce speaks of "an upsurge of interest and activity in the commercial port operation" - but that is centred down-river at Newham, and will be seen a little later in the walk.

Truro as seen from the Truro School area, probably during the late 1850s, shortly before the railway viaducts were built. Notice the various smelting-house chimneys; boats moored at what is now the Lemon Quay car park; and St Mary's Church, the Cathedral's predecessor.

in competition with the developing settlement of Truro. This "dangerous rivalry", as H.L.Douch calls it (BT), ended in 1300 when Thomas de Pridyas bought half of Truro. On the left are "prestigious developments", all built since I wrote *A View from Carn Marth;* they occupy the area where once stood Newham Station, and the older building which has been incorporated into "Vivian House", the Midland Bank's premises, probably originally belonged to the railway company. The mansion on the hill above is Newham House, built by R.A.Daniell of Trelissick, who was appointed Sheriff of Cornwall in 1795 (see the later note on the Mansion House); from about 1891 to 1909 it housed the Old Truro Grammar School, which then became Truro Cathedral School and moved to the Cathedral Close. You now pass beside various small industrial premises, including Cornish Calcified Seaweed (*). Up on the right almost opposite that is the GPO's new sorting office, officially opened by Princess Diana early in 1991. Somewhere nearby must have stood the Newham Smelting Works (*); no-one seems to know its exact site. Continue straight ahead between the side-walls of a former railway-bridge, beside Little Newham house and past Channel Foods to look at Lighterage Quay, from where tin ore was till recently still shipped. The large warehouse is owned by Truro Wharfage, who handle big import and export cargoes.

CALCIFIED SEAWEED

On the bottom in the deep water of Falmouth Bay are thick layers of dead *maerl*, a type of alga, which form a coral-like mass. This "calcified seaweed" is dredged and brought to Newham to be dried, crushed and bagged for use as a soil conditioner. Much of it goes to the St Austell area to help with the grassing-over of old china-clay spoil heaps.

NEWHAM SMELTING-HOUSE

Truro and its immediate surroundings were an important centre for tin-smelting. Up to the end of the 17th century, this was done in blowing-houses, so called because of the use of bellows, driven by a water-wheel, to raise the heat in the furnaces. In 1702, Robert Lydall took out a patent for a new technique using coal and anthracite instead of wood and charcoal, and dispensing with the bellows. The first use of the new "reverberatory furnace" in tin smelting was at Newham, where Lydall set up a smelting-house with ten such furnaces, in partnership with the aptly-named Francis Moult. "This was the first true smelting-house in Cornwall", says D.B.Barton in ECMH. The Newham works had several warehouses, a smithy, an office and other buildings, all surrounded by a high wall: secrecy was important - the workforce lived on the premises, and the manager kept firearms in his room. There was much opposition from blowing-house owners, who tried to prove that the new process produced inferior tin, but when tests were made by the Mint Office in 1708 no significant difference could be found. In 1711 the company built a new works at Calenick, apparently because of a lack of running water at Newham, and by about 1715 the Newham smelting-house had closed.

2 Return to Channel Foods, turn left up Lighterage Hill, and after a few yards take the path on the left, where there is a notice prohibiting firearms. You are now on the track of the old Newham branch line (*), and after a short cutting in which the right-hand side has become a sort of natural rock-garden, you have trees on your left, with glimpses of Calenick Creek (colour picture 23) - an amazing contrast on a working day to the clanking cranes and Industrial Estate traffic a few hundred yards back. After nearly a mile you reach a road.

THE NEWHAM BRANCH LINE

In 1852 the West Cornwall Railway opened its line from Penzance to Truro; the original terminus was at Highertown, but in 1855 the line was extended to Newham. When the Cornwall Railway, linking Truro to Plymouth, built Truro Station in 1859, the West Cornwall trains were mostly diverted there, and the Newham section became a branch line, carrying only goods after 1863, but was not closed down until 1971.

3 Turn left to visit Calenick village (*), which is attractive as well as having an important place in Cornwall's industrial history. The clock tower of the old smelting house is on the right; unfortunately, the high wall makes for problems in seeing any of the other buildings. On the left just before the bridge is the toll-house (this road was once the Falmouth-Truro turnpike!); notice, near the phone-box opposite, the Victorian post-box. Over the bridge, the first house on the right (River Cottage) was one of several pubs in Calenick in its industrial heyday; and beyond that is the former corn mill. From here, either return straight away up the road to the path along the railway track, following the directions from point 4; or for a pleasant short diversion, turn left past the terraced cottages, known as Ropewalk Row for a reason that will emerge later. After a couple of hundred yards turn left between wooden and stone gate-posts into a field, then follow the line of the footpath diagonally to a gate at the edge of woodland. Continue through this till it brings you down to the creek - an attractive picnic-spot with a pretty view of the village. You also see the salt-marsh through which the stream now winds; before the silting-up, caused largely by mining inland, the creek was tidal and navigable, as shown by the remains of quay walls at this point. In the small copse by the stream-bank just beyond the fence are a few hummocks and the base of an old wall: here once stood the limekiln which was being described by the old person quoted in the note about limekilns in Walk 10. The open field beyond was once woodland, and through it ran the Rope Walk, which also extended into the wood beyond, where its course can still be traced. This is where ropes were spun, and it is said that several of the old ropes were found underneath the limekiln when it was demolished. Now return to the railway-track path by the same route.

4 Turn left through the gate back on to the railway track heading north-east. Soon on the right you pass a brick shed - one of two apparently used as gravel stores for the railway. Below on the left, beside the embankment, you may be able to make out the course of the leat that once served the smelting works. By this point, the traffic on the A39 will almost certainly be all-too-audible; soon a railway bridge takes you across the road, and peace

CALENICK AND ITS SMELTING-HOUSE

The name, spelt "Carlinick" on Martyn's map (1748), probably derives from Cornish, *clunyek,* "marshy place". In 1711, when the Calenick smelting-house was built, Calenick Creek was navigable at least as far as Magor's Quay (the one at the end of the diversion described in section 3 of the directions), so that coal could be delivered there. Silting increased rapidly after that, mainly because of slime coming from the Wheal Jane area: in 1877, for example, it is estimated that 10,000 tons was deposited in the creek and Truro river from the Calenick stream alone. Even so, the smelting-house was the most successful of all the early ones in this area, and did not close down until 1891. In the yard was a workshop where crucibles were made, pieces of which can still be found in the creek. For more information about Calenick, including old maps, see the "project pack" mentioned in the note on limekilns, Walk 10.

gradually returns, to match the tranquillity of the valley scenery. Somewhere down there flows the little River Tinny, as Mr Brian Cock of Goodern Manor Farm (Walk 1) told me it was called; perhaps easier to discern, at least in winter, is the spire of Kea Church among the trees on the far side of the valley. This is the second of two churches to have been built on that site in the 19th century, replacing the 15th century parish church at Old Kea. (See *Around the Fal,* Walk 4.) A little further along, the woodland closer at hand is Nansavallan ("apple-orchard valley") Woods: again see Walk 1. About a mile past the first bridge is another crossing a country road near Treyew (*).

THE TREYEW SMELTING-HOUSE

There was an old blowing-house at Treyew; its owner (or, more accurately, managing partner) at the end of the 17th century, Samuel Enys, with help from Robert Lydall, converted it at a cost of £520 for the use of reverberatory furnaces like those at Newham and Calenick; the new smelting-house was in action by 1713. The business survived a law-suit brought by Moult of Calenick for breach of patent, but by 1760 was in a run-down condition, and seems to have closed before 1770. There appears to be no trace left now of Treyew Smelting House, but the former corn mill has survived.

5 Immediately after this, turn right, and then at the lane turn left. This takes you round behind New County Hall. Look back for a good view of Penweathers Junction, where the Falmouth Branch leaves the main London-Penzance line. Unfortunately you now have to cross the main road - no easy matter, but probably the safest place to do so is beside the roundabout on your right. Then turn left and immediately right along Dobbs Lane. Notice the main line in the cutting on the right, then the railway station with Old County Hall just beyond. On the skyline further right is another imposing granite building, the former Girls' Grammar School, now the Truro Sixth Form Centre. In 1991 this was threatened with demolition to make way for another huge supermarket; when the planning authority insisted that the existing building be incorporated in the scheme, Sainsbury's lost interest. The road curves downhill and becomes Bosvigo Lane, which takes its name from the nearby Bosvigo House (*). As you reach the Kenwyn River you will

BOSVIGO

The original house on this site probably dated from the 13th century; that was replaced in the 18th, when it belonged to Henry Rosewarne, who was much involved in local tin smelting, and in his latter years "was ready to try and overthrow the power of the Boscawens in Truro" (see TEC, page 21). Following his death in 1783 Bosvigo was acquired by the Lemon family of Carclew: see the later notes on the Mansion House and Princes House. There is now a Nursery in its grounds. The enclosed and walled gardens, woodland walk and Victorian conservatory are opened to the public on selected days in aid of charity: for details, see the current issue of the *Gardens of Cornwall Open Guide.* (During 1991, the garden will be open daily from June to September, and teas will be available. Dogs are not permitted.)

see a road and path signposted to Coosebean on the left; Coosebean was the site of another smelting house. (For an attractive walk in that direction see *The Landfall Book of Truro.)* Cross the bridge and turn right along St George's Road. As you pass under the railway viaduct, notice the stumps of Brunel's original structure on the far side, and then turn right to inspect the old building now partly occupied by the Truro Tyre Co. This was the Carvedras Smelting Works (*). If you go a few yards up the lane beside it and look into the yard on the right you will see it from the point where the photographer stood in 1893 when he took the picture reproduced in the drawing. Notice the wooden superstructure of the old viaduct. One of the granite moulds into which the molten tin was poured has been used as the base of a buttress in the lane; it is half-buried by the road now.

THE CARVEDRAS SMELTING-HOUSE

Carvedras had a blowing-house in the 18th century; reverberatory furnaces were added, probably before 1750. It continued in use until 1898. Several interesting photographs of it taken in the 1890s have been published, and it is the only smelting-house building within the city to have survived more-or-less intact.

Carvedras Smelting Works, Truro, in 1893

THE LEATS

The leat powered the Town Mill (flour and grist), which was situated on St Nicholas Street close to what is now Victoria Square, and a fulling-mill (for the scouring and cleaning of woollen cloth) owned by a Mr Tippet, whose name is preserved in a narrow passageway called Tippet's Backlet. The leat now helps to supply the water flowing along the gutters in the city streets, an unusual feature which was described in 1865 as "conducing to the general salubrity of the town." (Incidentally, it's worth your while to go down Tippet's Backlet, or any of the other passages on the right, to River Street and visit the County Museum, which has many exhibits of interest to the "industrial archaeologist".)

6 Now return to the viaduct, cross St George's Road, and follow the sign to Victoria Gardens. Walk with the Kenwyn River on your left at first, then cross to the other side beside a sluice-gate (colour picture 24). Now the river is on your right and a leat on your left; you are coming into the area known as The Leats (*). Continue along the alleyway by the river, crossing Edward Street and Castle Street. Look up to the left to see the new Courts of Justice, built on the probable site of the Norman castle. After Castle Street, keep heading towards the Cathedral. The river and leat are now underground, and it is this area and especially Victoria Square beyond that was particularly badly hit by flooding in 1988. A small dam has now been built at New Mill as a safeguard against such floods. Leading both right and left are several narrow passageways, known in Truro as "opes" (usually pronounced "opps"), although to me they were always "twittens" until my recent visit to York, since when they have been "snickelways". Perhaps "snopeltwitways" will do as the sort of compromise that pleases nobody. Anyway, turn left on any one of them: Pydar Mews, Coombes Lane, Nalder's Court or Tonkin's Ope, and you will soon reach High Cross, overshadowed by the west end of the Cathedral. The old cross which has recently been set up on a tall column was discovered in a nearby sewage-trench. In the mid-18th century, the cross that stood here had an iron ring in it, to which a bull was tethered. The animal was ridden down from Castle Hill by a dustman, fastened to the ring, "and then the tanners and fellmongers brought their dogs to bait it." (TEC). Turn left along the street on the south side of the Cathedral (*), right into the snopeltwitway now called Cathedral Lane, and left at the main street, named Boscawen Street, Boscawen being the family name of the Earls of Falmouth, whose estates include so much of Truro. The Victorian "Gothick" building at the end is built on the site of the old Coinage Hall (*). Walk up to this and take the right fork, where you will now pass the

TRURO CATHEDRAL

The Cathedral, built at the end of the 19th century, has a small green spire in addition to the three large ones. Whether or not it beautifies the building, it is of interest in being constructed of copper as a tribute to the importance of the Cornish mines. The side of the Cathedral that the walk takes you by is the only ancient part of it, being a remnant of St Mary's Church.

THE COINAGE HALL

Since the 14th century Truro had been one of the coinage towns. Twice a year, officials from London came to the Coinage Hall to test the quality of tin ingots by striking off a corner or "coign"; duty was levied, which went to the Duchy of Cornwall; the tin was then marked by the coinage-hammer and could be sold - although, as B.Trevail points out in *Curious Cornwall* (Tor Mark Books), much tin was smuggled out of the county untaxed. "At coinage time in Truro and Penzance," he writes, "huge blocks of tin, too heavy to be stolen, littered all the principal streets, with pack animals and carriers' carts coming and going from the coinage hall and the surrounding smelting houses." On the upper floor of the Coinage Hall regular Stannary Courts were held, and occasional Stannary Parliaments (Latin, *stannum,* tin). The rights of the tinners to govern their own affairs date back to 1197 and have been jealously guarded in Cornwall; the Parliament, meeting then at its oldest seat, Lostwithiel, created a stir as recently as 1974 by making an official protest to the Soviet Ambassador about Russian fishing boats "poaching" Cornish fish stocks. In the same year the Parliament approved the issue of special Cornish banknotes - including notes for five and ten shillings, since the Stannary Parliament had never sanctioned decimalisation! A recent attempt to use Stannary laws as a means of avoiding payment of Poll Tax has received much publicity.

THE MANSION HOUSE

The Mansion House was built about 1760 by the London architect Thomas Edwards, using Bath stone for most of the frontage, for Thomas Daniell. Daniell had been chief clerk to Sir William Lemon (see the next note); partly because of marrying into money, he was able to buy up the Lemon mining interests on Sir William's death. His son, Ralph Allen Daniell, was nicknamed "Guinea-a-minute" because this was said by Richard Polwhele to have been his income from one mine alone. (The Mansion House, by the way, was a wedding present from Mrs Daniell's uncle, who owned a quarry near Bath. Cynics have claimed that his intention was to advertise his product, and that as a result Bath stone was later used on many of the houses in Lemon Street; in fact, however, Mr Anthony Cartwright tells me that tests he has carried out show they are faced with elvan quarried at Newham. Mr Cartwright is the author of an interesting leaflet about the types of stone used in Truro Cathedral.

Mansion House (*) and Princes House (*) on the right, and on the left just before the by-pass road, the Old Mansion House (*). Walk back a few yards and take the right fork (Quay Street), back towards the Cathedral, then right into New Bridge Street. Immediately after crossing the bridge over the River Allen, turn right, under the archway of Highshore House, to walk by the river, with Enys Quay on the opposite side. On the left are the factory buildings formerly used by Furniss's, manufacturers of sweets and biscuits; "Furniss Island", which you are now on, is said to have been created by centuries of garbage. At the main road use the subway, and on the far side turn right, crossing both the rivers and returning to the car park.

PRINCES HOUSE

Princes House was designed about twenty years earlier by the same architect for William Lemon, and is also faced with Bath stone. Notice the rather more decorative style that was in fashion then. The entrance porch was added in the 1880s. Inside, there are fine balustrades and fireplaces and much magnificent plasterwork. The house once had a garden leading down to "Back Quay" on the River Kenwyn (see the photograph on page 69 of BT); part of it is now the site of the Creation Centre. Born in 1696, William Lemon as a young man became manager of a smelting works. In the 1720s he was the first to use Newcomen's steam pumping engine in Cornwall. The bulk of his fortune was made from copper mining, and at his death he left £300,000 - a vast sum when translated into modern values. A vivid little pen-portrait of William Lemon is given in TEC (pages 20-1). His country home was Carclew, overlooking Devoran and Restronguet Creek (Walk 11); this, too, was designed for him by Thomas Edwards.

THE OLD MANSION HOUSE

The Old Mansion House was the town house of Samuel Enys, and seems to have been built between 1706 and 1713 - so each of these three great houses in turn takes us a little further back in time. Enys inherited a large sum from his grandfather; with it he bought the Manor of Kenwyn and Truro, and also a large number of shares in mines. See also above for his involvement with Treyew smelting-house. (Incidentally, the grandfather just mentioned was Henry Gregor, whose family built "The Great House", later called Blackford's, on the corner next to Princes House. This is the oldest of all Truro's grand houses, but it was badly damaged by fire in 1920. Extensive renovation, amounting almost to a complete rebuilding, has been carried out to it since *Carn Marth* was published.)

For a detailed study of all these buildings and many more, see the excellent series of large-format booklets recently produced by the Truro Buildings Research Group, which are well illustrated by Christine Oates. The volume on Princes Street and the Quay Area is particularly relevant here. Christine Oates's The Truro City Trail *(Dyllansow Truran, 1984) gives only brief comments, but is an attractive pocket guide.*

LANNER, TRESAVEAN AND THE HAYLE RAILWAY

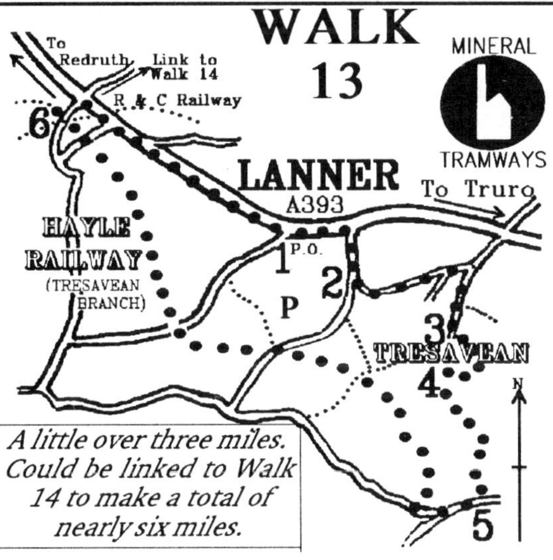

A little over three miles. Could be linked to Walk 14 to make a total of nearly six miles.

Of all the walks I am now adding to the original eight in *A View from Carn Marth,* this is the one which most obviously ought to have been included. It is very rich in historical importance: Lanner is an excellent example of a rural hamlet suddenly transformed into a quite sizeable mining community; Tresavean was among the top ten copper mines in Cornwall in terms of total output, and in 1838 was the third largest producer in the county; and much of the walk follows the track of a mineral railway which competed with the Redruth and Chasewater. The walk also offers some of the best views of any in the book, particularly of Carn Marth itself, but also right across Cornwall from south coast to north. The going is mostly easy, along tracks and minor roads, with just one short stretch on footpaths; at the end there is over half a mile on a main road, but a pavement runs the whole way along it. It is quite a hilly area, and there is a little climbing to do near the start, but most of the walk, being on an old railway line, is level. Lanner has several shops, and the Lanner Inn is very handily located next to the recommended parking-place. Another good parking spot is indicated by **P** on the map.

Directions are given from the village square in Lanner (*), which is on the right just before you reach the post office if you are approaching from Redruth. To drive there from Truro, you could take the A390 to Threemilestone, forking left there through Chacewater and Carharrack and turning right on reaching the A393 Falmouth/Redruth road; alternatively, follow the directions at the start of Walk 7, again turning right at the A393. In both these cases you will find the parking place on your left.

1 Start by walking eastwards along the main road - that is, towards Penryn/Falmouth, past the post office. Turn right at Bell Lane, whose name probably has nothing to do with bells but may derive from Cornish *pell,* distant; a nearby farm is called Bell Veor, veor meaning "great". What looks almost like a castle wall on the left was apparently once part of the boundary of a farm's walled garden. Next comes a modern school building.

2 Just beyond that, turn left on to a pretty lane signposted to Bell Veor. Ignore the lane on the right to Tresavean Farm; continue almost until you are

LANNER

The name, often seen in old books as "Lannarth", means "clearing". Oliver Padel refers to four other places in Cornwall with the same name, plus others derived from the same Cornish original; plainly, Cornwall must once have been much more thickly wooded than it is now. This particular Lanner is a good example, because there is evidence that Carn Marth was at least partially tree-covered until the rapid expansion of mining in the 18th century, with its heavy demands for charcoal and timber. "Back in the 13th century," writes Sheila Bird in BCV, "the Bishop of Exeter had enclosed the woodland of his manor here to create a deer park." I don't know what evidence Ms Bird has for this statement, and I wonder if she has confused this Lanner with the one in St Allen parish, just north of St Clement Woods. According to Charles Henderson in ECH, Bishop Bronescombe set up deer parks there, at Pawton near Wadebridge and at Glasney, Penryn (see Walk 5 - the note on College and Argal Reservoirs). "At the present day," remarks Henderson, "the extensive coppice wood of 300 acres called Bishop's Wood remains to mark the park of Lanner." (See *The Landfall Book of Truro* for a walk in that area.) But I think we can be sure C.C.James had got the correct Lanner when he wrote in HPG, "Before 1800, it is said to have contained only six cottages and the road from Redruth being so little frequented, Francis says it was regarded with fear by women and youth." With the traffic roaring past (who cares about speed limits?) it's almost impossible now to picture Lanner as a woodland clearing, but you don't have to go many yards along the side-roads before finding farms and pretty countryside. As one of the typical car-drivers who hurry through the main street, I was amazed how much more interesting and even attractive it was when I got out and walked. The long rows of miners' cottages stand cheek-by-jowl with old farm buildings, large chapels and apparently deserted mansions, and among them run numerous paths and passageways to little back-streets and the fields and hills.... The terraces began to be built about 1830, in response to the success of the mines, especially Tresavean, and the former dependence of the community on mining seems to be neatly symbolised in James's statement that "the stream flowing through the village originates from an Adit in Penstruthal Mine." "As tin prices increased in the early nineteen hundreds," writes Mrs J.A.P.Hopkins in a brief account of Lanner's history, "Tresavean mine was re-opened, and miners poured into the village from surrounding areas, looking for work. Residents today recollect the large number of men trudging through the village each day, in their big heavy boots, and the teams of four horses pulling carts full of tin across the hill, to the top of Lanner Hill, on its way to the smelting house at Bassett."

back to the main road, but then turn right, up Tresavean Hill, and continue straight on past Tresavean Flats, where you join a stony, uphill track.

3 Take the second turning on the left, which brings you to the ruins of the famous old Tresavean mine (*). Kenneth Brown has kindly given me the following account of recent work on this site. "Early in 1991 a shaft-capping and landscaping programme was carried out despite opposition by

TRESAVEAN MINE

T.A.Morrison's very detailed account of Tresavean's history in CCM suggests that it was active in 1700, and mentions that a steam engine was working there as early as 1758. It ended as a tin mine, but as I mentioned in the introductory note, it was one of the leading producers during the heyday of the Gwennap copper mines: Collins in OWEMR states that its sales of copper ore between 1815 and 1856 amounted to £1,344,227. (The following 13 years, however, according to C.C.James in HPG, yielded only £14,975.) The first "man-engine" ever used in Britain, to relieve miners of the need to use ladders, was installed at Tresavean in 1842 ; it must have been especially welcome in view of the high underground temperatures (86°F at 264 fathoms, as measured in 1843). James states that the Royal Cornwall Polytechnic Society gave a prize to its inventor, Michael Loam, and helped pay for the installation to a depth of 200 fathoms (1,200 feet). A man-engine was , however, in use in the Harz mining region of Germany from 1833, and a similar principle was employed to raise ore to surface as long ago as 1694 in Sweden, so perhaps Mr Loam was rather lucky to get his prize. (For the fullest account of the history of the man-engine, see CBE. Eventually 16 were used in Cornwall.) Morrison tells the story of how a young barrow-boy working at Tresavean, William Martin, noticed a rich lode of copper. "From poverty," as *The Mining Journal* put it, "the mine was soon after stopped." When, nearly twenty years later in 1817, Martin returned as the mine's manager he exploited his boyhood discovery, and the statistics of the mine's output of copper ore speak for themselves: 1817: 139 tons; 1818: 497 tons; 1819: 2,156 tons. He continued as manager for over forty years, became owner of one of the grandest houses in Stithians, Crellow House, and two thousand people attended his funeral in 1861. Morrison calculates that at the mine's peak of prosperity, in the mid-1830s, "the owner of one share would have received in modern terms a tax-free income of £600,000 a year." Like so many other large mines, Tresavean was a combination of several setts which at certain periods worked independently: H.G.Dines in MMR lists Bellvean Mine, Wheal Comford, Tretharrup, Treviskey, Trethellan, Brewer and West Trethellan. Most of these names appear on the OS Pathfinder map, and they give some idea of the extent of the workings; Dines prints a diagram of the main underground workings, showing how the deepest shaft penetrated to 395 fathoms (nearly 2,400 feet) to reach the tin which lies below the copper. This was the level reached in 1923, during the mine's last period of activity; falling tin prices led to final closure in 1928, by which time a depth of 2,660 feet had been attained, making Tresavean the second deepest mine in Cornwall. (The deepest was Dolcoath, Camborne, where the 3,000-foot Williams Shaft was sunk before the turn of the century.) If not quite the deepest, it was certainly the tallest when in 1907 the chimney of the pumping-engine house was raised to 150 feet in order to create the draught needed by the three big new boilers for the steam-engines that drove the electric pumps. (Tresavean was "the first mine in the county to be unwatered by electric turbine pumps," according to James.) Four photographs showing Tresavean at this period are in MC.

local historians and the County's own archaeologists. Increasing interest in Cornwall's industrial past suggests that this may be the very last "scorched earth" project carried out: one certainly hopes so. The declared aim was to tidy up the results of illegal dumping and turn the mine into the kind of amenity the village needs, as well as recognising its historical importance. Time will tell how successful the planners have been. One "plus" factor was the discovery while scavenging the burrows of parts of a wooden-beam engine and of a flat-rod pivot used when pumping from a remote shaft. These relics are probably pre-1800 and have been rescued for display in a future mining museum. Some splendid samples of malachite and other copper ores were also exposed to view. The only beam engine house still standing contained a stamps engine but was mutilated this century to turn it into a transformer house. The house of a modern horizontal winding engine (built in Scotland!), dating from about 1920, has also escaped destruction, as has the mouth of Man-Engine shaft because it is home to a rare bat species." Follow the track as it curves first to the right, past some caravans, and then left, where the splendid view of Carn Marth is replaced by an even wider vista across United Downs to china-clay country. Continue winding uphill as far as a rusty wrought-iron gate (on your right).

Tresavean Mine: ruined engine house. Pennance Mine and Carn Marth in the background.

4 At that point take the track on the left, where the view is best of all, stretching from Pennance Mine engine house on the left side of Carn Marth to Carrick Roads (identifiable, when we did this walk, by an oil-rig) and the sea horizon, and embracing St Day church, Carharrack, and Consolidated and United Mines. The track takes you past Lower Tretharrup, whose name means either "very pleasant farm" or "unpleasant farm". The frantic barking of what sounded like hundreds of mastiffs thirsting for human blood as we approached led us to the latter interpretation, but luckily they were all inside securely closed buildings. Half-buried among brambles was an elderly farm-implement, perhaps for sowing seeds. Ignore the track going left soon after that.

5 At the road turn right, at the junction a little later keep right, and then take the signed path on the right just after that. Cross the stile and walk with the hedge on your left. The gap in the hedge ahead was overgrown, so we went though the gateway on the right. Cross the stone cattle-grid at the following field corner, and continue ahead to the low stile at the next corner, left of a metal gate. Now go left, along a slightly overgrown path between hedges which could possibly once have been part of the mineral railway system; there are no obvious granite setts, but mine tramways were usually narrow gauge with wooden sleepers. Soon this brings you to the top of the hill overlooking Lanner. Keep right of the electricity sub-station and ignore the tracks down to the right and up to the left; the path to look for is a few feet above the wider track. It starts near a big open shaft ("probably gone or going", says Kenneth Brown) up on the left, runs almost due west (that is, continuing in roughly the direction you came) and is fairly level. Once you have found it you will be in no doubt, because it is the course of the Tresavean Branch of the Hayle Railway (*), and it is marked by a well-preserved double line of granite setts with bolt-holes where the rails were attached to them. Some still have projecting iron spikes, so you need to walk with care. Within the next half-mile-or-so the railway track crosses two roads, either of which would return you quite quickly to Lanner if you want to cut the walk short; to get to the second one you would need to go down a fairly steep path on the left beside the bridge. After that the line, now heading north, runs through a cutting - rather soggy underfoot in October - and then comes a fine open stretch. At the next road, still continue ahead past works buildings and a dome-covered reservoir till you reach yet another road. This is the point at which the Redruth and Chasewater Railway's branch line to Wheal Buller (*) crossed the Hayle Railway - a crossing which, says D.B.Barton in RCR, "was unprotected by gates or any form of signal". Relics still remain of the storage yards both railways had at this point. Cross the road and go a few yards further along the Tresavean

THE HAYLE RAILWAY

The Hayle Railway opened in 1837, linking Hayle, with its important harbour, smelting works and foundries, to Camborne, Redruth and Portreath (see *A View from Carn Brea* for details about the Incline there), with branches to Crofty, Roskear and Tresavean. It was principally a mineral line, but also carried passengers on some sections; and it was worked mainly by locomotives, except below the steep inclines at Angarrack and Portreath. Locomotives worked up the incline to Wheal Uny on the Tresavean branch, but according to D.B.Barton horses worked the line from there to Tresavean. The "standard gauge" (4ft. 8.5in.) was used. In 1846 the Hayle Railway was taken over by the West Cornwall Railway, who by 1852 extended it to reach Penzance and Truro; passenger traffic increased, but the mainstay of business was still the minerals trade until the serious recession of the 1870s. Eventually the West Cornwall was absorbed by larger companies, and the whole system was finally taken over by the GWR in 1889. The Tresavean branch continued in use till the 1930s.

WHEAL BULLER

This was another old and rich copper mine; in conjunction with Wheal Beauchamp (pronounced "Beecham"), its total output, as recorded in CMCD, slightly exceeded that of Tresavean. Its most successful period was 1848-54, when "the adventurers in Wheal Buller were the envy of the mining world," since this was a period of depression in the mining industry generally; "the company could hardly distribute its profits fast enough" (CCM). Those profits were greatly assisted by the fact that rich copper lodes were at comparatively shallow depths, so that the workings were easy to reach and pumping and winding expenses were light. In the earlier part of the 19th century Wheal Buller was under the control of John Taylor. Surprisingly, perhaps, he had not linked it to his mineral railway, the Redruth and Chasewater. When new adventurers took the mine over in 1848, they made the connection, and in 1849 the railway's directors bought the branch line for £85 - an investment which, as Barton says, "in the years to come was to prove money well spent" (RCR). The line extended to the far side of the Helston - Redruth road, where a storage yard similar to the Great Yard near Carharrack (Walk 3) was built. (Barton believes the line may have eventually reached Wheal Basset Stamps near Carnkie and thus linked with the Basset tramway: see *A View from Carn Brea,* Walk 10.) Despite what Barton describes as "spirited attempts" from about 1860 onwards to turn Wheal Buller into a tin producer, the mine closed in 1875, and efforts to restart it in 1881-5, 1888, 1908-10 and 1928-30 came to nothing. There is very little of the mine left to see on the surface, apart from the many shafts on Buller Downs, between Lanner and Four Lanes.

line, and suddenly a totally new view opens up, of the twin engine houses of Wheal Uny, Carn Brea and the sea horizon to the north. The Tresavean trackway continues, beyond a metal gate, westwards for a mile or so, and then the line curved north to descend a rope-worked incline and join the main London-Penzance line just west of Redruth.

6 Return to the road now and turn left, then right on the main road. *(Or, to link into Walk 14, cross the main road with great care when you reach it and continue ahead on the track opposite, Carn Marth Lane. At the T-junction go right, and soon you come to the Pennance Mine engine house, on the route of Walk 14.)* Luckily, there's a pavement all the way along the main road into Lanner. After about a hundred yards, just below the brow of the hill, you will come to the point at which the Redruth and Chasewater line crossed the road: its course is marked by a wall on the left beside an electricity-supply pole and on the right beside a crossroads sign. As you descend into Lanner, notice the strange mixture of houses and other buildings, old and new, neglected and spruce, urban and rural. If they ever build a bypass for Lanner it could be a pleasant place to live; unfortunately, almost any possible alternative route for the main road would destroy peaceful countryside and much of historical importance.

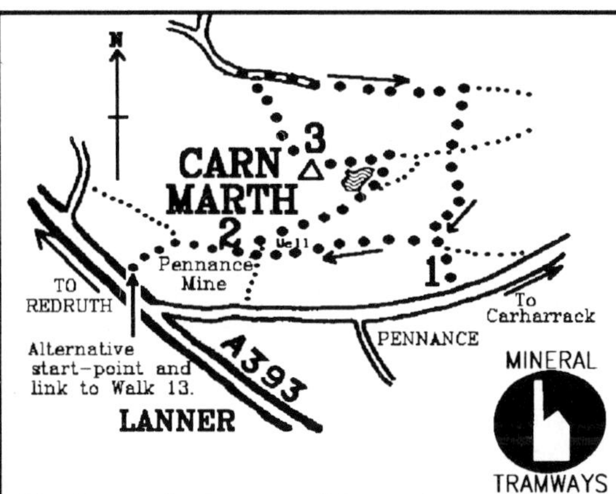

WALK 14
CARN MARTH

About two and a half miles

Colour pictures 25 & 26

A short walk unless you link it with the previous one, and not strenuous, but there are one or two steepish slopes, and waterproof footwear is advisable. It makes an ideal conclusion to this series of walks by providing a marvellous panorama, not only of pretty-well the whole region covered in this book, but also of neighbouring areas that beckon the explorer. To the north is St Agnes Beacon, to the west Carn Brea, to the south the Fal, to the east - visible at least to the mind's eye! - Newquay, Fowey and Padstow....

To drive to the starting-point from Truro, follow the directions to Chacewater at the start of Walk 2; continue through the village and fork left for St Day; turn left on the main road (B3298) before you reach the centre of St Day. In about one mile this goes through Carharrack, past Railway Terrace (see Walk 3). As you approach the far side of Carharrack, fork right on to the (unsignposted) minor road which passes the restored footbridge over the Redruth and Chasewater Railway track. Continue along this road for about a mile, until you come to a group of houses on the left, whose names include Carn Villas, Glen-View and Peke-Yetu. You should be able to park here - as close to the walls as possible, please, and without blocking anyone's entrance. For an alternative parking space, continue till you reach the main road (A393), turn right on that, and after about two hundred yards turn right again on to a track. This is immediately before the road descends Lanner Hill, and almost opposite the Lanner Hill Garage. A notice states that this is a private road, open to the public only as a footpath and bridleway, but careful parking at the start of it should present no problems, so long as you bear in mind that the track is used by large lorries. From there walk up the track to the engine house and pick up the directions at point 2.

1 Starting at the first parking-place mentioned above, go up the public footpath opposite Carn Villas, keeping straight on as it becomes quite steep - grassy at first, but muddy before long, I'm afraid. At the wider track, turn left, then left again. The village below on the left now is Lanner (see the note in Walk 13). After the quarry on your left (which may be the one where china clay was once mined), ignore the path on the right going uphill; pass through the gateway in a granite wall and go to the right of the farm gate; beyond this the path continues between hedges and heads for an engine house. It's a rather fine one which contained a 50-inch pumping engine in the 1870s; notice the Count House just beyond, where mine business would have been transacted. The mine, once called Wheal Amelia and later Pennance ("head of the valley", the name of the hamlet on the south side of Carn Marth), was a surprisingly small one in view of the prominence of its engine house: the only records of production to have survived are of 590 tons of copper ore and a little tin between 1866 and 1872. The mine's nickname, "Wheal Bloody Nose", suggests that those who invested heavily in it had a nasty shock. In August 1990 *The West Briton* reported that the engine house was "in urgent need of repair to stop it falling down" and that its owner was willing to offer it to the local authorities. The possibility that the long-term preservation of the building might be part of the Mineral Tramways Project was mentioned.

2 From the engine house take the uphill track sharp right (left, of course, if you have approached from the second parking-place). After about 200 yards, immediately before a row of granite boulders on the right side of the track begins, there is a small triangular patch of rough ground slightly below the level of the track on the right. This is the location of a "holy well" known as Figgy Dowdy's or Margery Daw's Well. "Figgy Dowdy had a well," according to the local saying, "On the top of Carn Marth Hill, And she locked it night and day Lest people should carry the water away." J.Meyrick in HWC describes it as "an ancient and imposing granite structure with beehive roof and steps leading down to the cold and crystal water." That was in 1980; the eleven years since then seem to have wrought changes, since concrete blocks and various bits of metal now get in the way, but still the steps lead down and still the water is clear. A few yards further up the track is a disused granite quarry in which an open-air theatre has been created by the Carn Marth Protection Group (formed in 1986 in response to proposals to restart blasting in this quarry). The first performance there, *The Three Musketeers* by Shiva Theatre in 1987, was lit by car headlamps; work on cutting seats out of the rock began by 1989. To compare it with Epidaurus may be a little fanciful, but it does share several design features with the ancient Greek and Roman theatres, and its small scale doesn't rob it of all impressiveness. The article about work on the quarry face is taken from *The West Briton,* 8th March 1990. The view to the south from the track near the mouth of the quarry is extensive, including Stithians reservoir and a long stretch of coastline, with Falmouth Docks and Pendennis prominent. At the top, walk round the flooded quarry-pit, which since I wrote *Carn Marth* has had assorted rubbish cleared out of it by the Protection Group, including three cars. (I happened to be driving along the A393 not so long ago when a helicopter was lifting one of them out.)

Hanging about making quarry safe

MIKE BRYANT spent much of Tuesday "hanging about", inside a steel cage at the end of a crane hawser, knocking off loose granite from a quarry face at Carn Marth.

An ex-Wheal Jane miner, 18 months ago he gave up underground work to join Carnon Contracting, of Pool, and he was part of the team making safe the quarry for Carn Marth Protection Group.

As Mike worked at one face, so Gary Lobb, of Lobb Bros, Summercourt, was using the bucket of his digger to knock large granite chunks off another.

And when they came to one 35-ton "wart" with cracks, it was the time to use explosive to ease it down to the quarry floor.

The men are working on a Kerrier Groundwork Trust project funded by a Department of the Environment reclamation grant to make the quarry safe.

Not only will their work help stop people accidentally falling over the edge, but will make the area safe for the protection group's annual theatrical presentation which draws hundreds to the quarry.

It is all part of a sensitive restoration of this wild heather-clad hilltop which will include removing old quarry building eyesores and stone heaps.

Pennance Mine, on the slopes of Carn Marth

Your view eastwards now reaches to the china-clay "mountains" around St Austell, and closer at hand is most of the area covered by Walks 1-13. The hill on the skyline north-east is St Agnes Beacon; closer in roughly the same direction is the Grambler & St Aubyn engine-house, and closer still, though hard to make out, Gwennap Pit. Carharrack and St Day are to the right of those. Walk on round to the trig. point; from there you can see the north coast; Carn Brea is the hill to the west, topped by the de Dunstanville Monument(1835) and Carn Brea Castle; and the town below is Redruth, with the stack of Pednandrea mine prominent. (Time for a commercial: walks exploring most of the area to the north and west are detailed in *A View from St Agnes Beacon* and *A View from Carn Brea;* see also *The Book of the Poldice Valley,* which includes a schematic guide to the view from Carn Marth.) Little evidence of prehistoric man remains on Carn Marth, but C.C.James in HPG says that three "large tumuli" stood at the top, and one Bronze Age barrow is still visible near the trig. point. A century before James's book, a *History of Gwennap* was written by William Francis, and he states that "The largest tumulus or barrow was opened in 1789 and two

British urns were found beneath the stones." The meaning of the hill's name (often written "Carnmarth") has been much debated. "Carn of King Mark" has its supporters, and would make a satisfying link with Walk 1; the 18th-century historian Tonkin refers to "a lofty mountain called Carnemark". But "Carn of horses" is more probable - compare Kilmarth, Daphne du Maurier's home near Fowey. The belief that Carn Marth was formerly covered with trees, mainly sessile oaks, has been confirmed by the discovery of roots, according to James. From ancient times the hill was used as a Beacon for Mayday and Midsummer Fires; in the 19th century the method was to set the gorse alight, so that in dry conditions the whole hill would have been ablaze, and if the mines didn't finish off all the trees, that did.

As you stand here, you may be interested to read part of the description of this view which George Henwood wrote in about 1858. (I'm not quite convinced that everything he claims to see actually is, or ever was, visible - but in any case his account vividly sums up much of what this book has been about, as well as being interesting to compare with Leifchild's words which I quoted at the start.)

"Within a radius of two miles from the spot on which you now stand, more than 20,000,000l. - aye, than 30,000,000l. - worth of minerals have been raised from the bowels of the earth, and have been wrought for generations. That narrow winding valley on the south-east was the scene of, perhaps, some of the earliest endeavours at mining ever practised in this country; its origin has been lost in oblivion; but certain it is the Carnon Stream, for that is its name, was wrought at a very remote period, possibly before the present race inhabited this island. Down this valley at your feet must once have rushed a mighty torrent, hurling a prodigious quantity of tin before its impetuous flood, thus providing an easy mode of procuring it, when man, from his imperfect knowledge of metallurgy and gun-powder, would have been unable to pierce the tremendously hard rocks he even now finds it difficult to explore. Wonderful Providence! Striking illustration of the order and contrivance in the works of the Deity! In working this stream ample evidence was discovered of the primitive races who sought tin here. The implements of work were wooden shovels, in a few instances shod with iron, showing how valuable a metal iron must have been then. Many picks formed of the horns of deer were discovered, as well as other contrivances of a rude construction. The ingenuity of the present age has not only enabled the tinner to rework the old men's refuse at a great profit, but to pursue his avocation beneath yon tidal river, where you observe a number of shipping. Yes, beneath the navy there, conveying coal to and carrying off the produce of the mines, works the tinner, at a depth of sixty feet, in silence and safety. That railway whose locomotive you may perceive runs to Devoran - watch it; see how it threads through the different mines with its immense burden!

"This group of engine-houses are the surface buildings of the United Mines: let us count - one, two, three, aye, seven engines in a small space. Those beyond, in the same line, are the Clifford Mines. Still further east are the Great Baddern, Wheal Jane, and East Falmouth. On the north of, parallel to and in immediate proximity, are the Great Consolidated Mines, with their ten enormous engines...."

.... And so he continues, listing at least another 25 mines in view.

(Incidentally, at about the same time as Henwood wrote that, a man who called himself "Captain Head" contributed a description of the Gwennap Mines as seen from Carn Marth to the *Edinburgh Review.* Parts of it are quoted in PC, pages 105-7, and Claude Berry's own response to the Gwennap landscape on the following pages also makes interesting reading.)

3 From the trig. point, return to the main track heading towards Redruth, passing a deep quarry on your right. The owner of this quarry has caused some controversy by seeking permission to build an office and workshop in it. Continue down to the road and turn right, past the quarry-entrance with rusty old machinery beside it. Walk straight on past the house. After nearly half a mile you come to a crossroads (or crosstracks), with two metal gates ahead; here turn right. Go straight on where another track crosses, near a ruined building. Turn left at the next path, and then bear right downhill to return to your car.

* * * * *

The main headline in *The West Briton* on the day I am typing this into my word-processor (7th March 1991) is: **It's over: No lifeline for mines.** But a letter inside says, "Cornish mining may be in a terminal state in its present form, but I am sure that it is not dead for ever." There have been too many false conclusions in the past for the people of Cornwall to accept that this really is final. Before you drive away from the Gwennap mines, perhaps it would be fitting to read the last words of Henwood's essay. They make a suitable ending to this book, as a reflection not only on what once was, but on what perhaps again may be.

".... that Cornwall [without her mines], instead of her present active, teeming population, and highly prosperous state, would have been a howling wilderness and a desert, her sons barbarians, and her gentry paupers - in short, that the mines of England are her main stay and safeguard, and that in this glorious category the mines of Cornwall form a principal and leading feature, and as such should be cherished and encouraged. The mines and miners deserve it, and God grant they may receive it."

A QUARRYMAN REMEMBERS

In mid-May 1991 I led a walk in the Kennall Vale at the request of the Kerrier Groundwork Trust. ("Gunpowder and Bluebells," the event was christened.) One member of the party who soon introduced himself to me was Mr Peter Penpraze. He now lives in Illogan and earns his living as a builder, but he started his working life at Richards' Quarry in the Kennall Vale and continued there for 15 or more years till it closed in 1965. In all the intervening 26 years he had never returned - not very surprising, since the site had been closed to the public for most of that time. It was obvious as we walked around that memories were flooding back and that he had many an interesting story to tell, so he and I arranged to meet at the Vale again a few days later, and this time he would be the guide.

The quarrying company, he told me, had started work during the last century on a site a little further east, and he believes they opened up the new quarry in Kennall Vale some time before the closure of the gunpowder works in 1914. Most of the work-force, which amounted to 30 or 40 men when he was there, came from Stithians, and they were nearly all related: calling a Cornishman "Cousin Jack" was more than just a figure of speech!

The first sizeable building on the left beyond the main entrance, marked as "Packing House" on my map, Mr Penpraze remembers as the quarry office where he queued for his pay every week. Its complete contents then consisted of a safe, a table and a chair. Not far beyond that, the remains of a thick granite wall on the left mark the place where granite chippings were fed to a vibrating sieve which graded them for size before they were shovelled on to lorries. A few yards past that on the right are some low structures which were built to carry the huge frame saw, where long, thin slabs of granite were cut for use as shop fronts and the like. The saw blade was about twelve feet long, a foot wide and a quarter of an inch thick; it did not have teeth, but small, sharp pieces of steel "shot" were fed underneath it as it moved, and water was poured on as the cutting proceeded. The saw cut about an inch per hour. The first of the ruined concrete buildings just beyond the frame saw were the polishing room and then the carborundum shop, where a carborundum saw was used to do the smaller, finer cutting jobs. Nearby, closer to the path, was the air compressor: compressed air was used for many purposes including drilling and pumping water out of the quarry. The compressor was powered by electricity generated in the small building beside it. On the left side of the path here can still be seen the narrow leat which carried the water pumped out of the quarry.

Most of the buildings Mr Penpraze mentioned next were flimsy "galvanize" structures which have now totally vanished. On the right, in an area now strewn with rough stone blocks, was the office of Mr W. Bowden, the foreman, where the men clocked in; near that was the lettering shop, where letters for headstones and the like were carved out and usually filled with lead, supplied in molten form by the blacksmith, Dick Andrew. The blacksmith's shop survives almost intact, complete with furnace and the remains of two water troughs.

Our tour had now brought us close to the quarry excavation itself. A few feet from it, on a concrete foundation still in place, was the main crane, with a 60-foot jib. Beside that (to the left as you face the flooded pit) were two tin sheds: one where the blocks were split by the plugging and feathering process for use as kerb stones and similar, and another, larger one where the blocks were chipped to shape. The quarry pit itself was 125 feet deep from the ridge on the far side, so the notice warning of deep water is no exaggeration. Mr Penpraze described in vivid detail the method by which the men - himself included - perched on a long ladder as they removed huge blocks of stone from the vertical face. The ladder was suspended from a large and - they firmly believed! - strongly-rooted tree growing beside the precipice, and the ends of the ropes by which it was hung were tied round the workman's waist in case he should slip off the ladder while drilling holes, sometimes as much as 15 feet deep, for blasting. Apparently, however, no-one ever did, and Mr Penpraze could recall no serious accident at the quarry apart from the occasion when a man carrying drills walked into a large block of granite dangling at head-height from the crane.

Beyond the quarry on the left side of the track is a tall, strong granite wall. Mr Penpraze thinks this dates back to the days of the gunpowder works, but it was very useful to the quarrymen, because they would, as he put it, "dive behind it" whenever blasting was taking place. Another relic of the gunpowder days which the quarry made use of was the upper half of the top pair of incorporating mills (No. 7 on the map), where a new waterwheel was installed, probably about 1925-30, to supply power for the quarry's first air compressor, housed within the mill. Parts of the wheel and gearing are still in place, as also is the iron or steel pipe by which the compressed air was brought to the quarry. Another member of the party I had conducted around the site, Mr Clifford, told me that his uncle had installed the compressor; the job had been completed on Christmas Eve, and the machine's working life had been launched by the singing of carols!

Visit the Kennall Vale in winter or early spring nowadays and you are likely to be impressed by the roar of wind in the treetops and of water in the river and gushing over the sides of the leats. What a different world this must have been little over 25 years ago when giant vibrating sieves, stone-cutting saws, pneumatic drills, generators, cranes and heavy lorries created an almost constant racket, punctuated by occasional explosions when the rock-face was blasted! Yet one of the points Mr Penpraze kept coming back to was, despite all that and the hard labour, the risks and the meagre pay, how happy everyone who worked at the quarry always seemed to be.

A granite block prepared for splitting by the plug-and-feather method. This block was about 5 feet long; the drilled holes were about 3 inches deep and the same distance apart.

BOOKS REFERRED TO IN THE WALKS DESCRIPTIONS

AC	David Mudd: About the City (Bossiney, 1979)
ASI	Always Something Interesting - Aspects of History in Stithians, compiled by members of the Stithians Local History Group (6 volumes so far, published bi-annually since 1980)
AWF	Sheila Bird: Around the Waterways of the Fal (privately published, 1988)
BBKS	F.W.Bourne: Billy Bray, the King's Son (written soon after Billy's death in 1868; modern editions published by the Epworth Press)
BCIS	R.D.Penhallurick: The Birds of Cornwall and the Isles of Scilly (Headland, 1978)
BCV	Sheila Bird: A Book of Cornish Villages (Dovecote, 1988)
BE	T.E.Crowley: Beam Engines (Shire, 1976/1982)
BOEC	Nikolaus Pevsner: The Buildings of England: Cornwall (Penguin, 1951)
BT	H.L.Douch: The Book of Truro (Barracuda Books, 1977)
CA	Cornish Archaeology, the annual journal of the Cornwall Archaeological Society
CBE	D.B.Barton: The Cornish Beam Engine (Bradford Barton, 1965, recently reprinted)
CCG	Charles Henderson: The Cornish Church Guide and Parochial History of Cornwall (1925; Bradford Barton, 1964)
CCM	T.A.Morrison: Cornwall's Central Mines, The Southern District, 1810-1895 (Alison Hodge, 1983)
C&CM	R.L.Atkinson: Copper and Copper Mining (Shire, 1987)
CE	Bryan Earl: Cornish Explosives (Trevithick Society, 1978)
CGCP	David Guthrie: The Complete Guide to Cornish Pubs (Half Pint Press, no date - probably 1989)
CIMM	J.R.Leifchild: Cornwall, Its Mines and Miners (1857, recently reprinted by Frank Cass)
COM	H.V.Williams: Cornwall's Old Mines (Tor Mark)
CMCD	D.B.Barton: A History of Copper Mining in Cornwall and Devon (Bradford Barton, 1961)
CMD	Cyril Noall: Cornish Mine Disasters (Truran, 1989)
CMH	Peter Stanier: Cornwall's Mining Heritage (Twelveheads, 1988)
CMM	George Henwood: Cornwall's Mines and Miners (1857-9, reprinted by Bradford Barton, 1972)
CN	T.F.G.Dexter: Cornish Names (1926, reprinted by Bradford Barton, 1968)
CPN	O.J.Padel: A Popular Dictionary of Cornish Place-Names (Alison Hodge, 1988)
CPNE	O.J.Padel: Cornish Place-Name Elements (English Place-Name Society, 1985)
CRH	John Stengelhofen: Cornwall's Railway Heritage (as CMH)
CSG	John Betjeman: Cornwall, A Shell Guide (Faber, 1964)

CW D.E.Benney: An Introduction to Cornish Watermills (Bradford Barton, 1972)

DD D. A.Kneebone:Deep as Dolcoath(privately published,1990)

DDCV Barry Simpson: Devoran, A Different Cornish Village (privately published, 1990)

ECH Charles Henderson: Essays in Cornish History (Bradford Barton, 1963)

ECMH D.B.Barton: Essays in Cornish Mining History (2 volumes) (Bradford Barton, 1968 & 1971)

FRV Ivy Edwards, with Rachel and Elisabeth Rowlands: The Family at Rose Villa (privately published, 1988)

HAF The Fal History Group: History Around the Fal (several volumes, the first published in 1980)

HCMSS J.H.Trounson: Historic Cornish Mining Scenes at Surface (Bradford Barton, no date)

HPG C.C.James: A History of the Parish of Gwennap (privately printed, no date - probably late 1940s)

HW P.O. & D.V.Leggatt: The Healing Wells (Truran, 1987)

HWC J.Meyrick: A Pilgrim's Guide to the Holy Wells of Cornwall (privately published, 1982)

IAC W.H.Curnow: Industrial Archaeology of Cornwall (Tor Mark)

IAC(2) A.C.Todd & Peter Laws: Industrial Archaeology of Cornwall (David & Charles, 1972)

JTS The Journal of the Trevithick Society, published annually

KCD ed. R.Maber & A.Tregoning: Kilvert's Cornish Diary (Alison Hodge, 1989)

KEC Arthur Mee: The King's England: Cornwall (Hodder, 1937)

LPH J.Polsue: Lake's Parochial History of the County of Cornwall (1867-73, republished in 1974 by EP Publishing Ltd.)

MC J.H.Trounson: Mining in Cornwall, Volume 2 (Moorland)

MCT C.G.Down: Mining in Cornwall Today (Cornish Chamber of Mines, 1974, plus later editions)

MMC A.K.Hamilton Jenkin: Mines and Miners of Cornwall (16 volumes published in the 1960s; some recently reprinted)

MMR H.G.Dines: The Metalliferous Mining Region of South-West England (2 volumes) (HMSO, 1956)

MSC Barry Atkinson: Mining Sites in Cornwall and South West Devon (Truran, 1988)

MTP Cornwall Archaeological Unit: The Mineral Tramways Project (Cornwall County Council, 1989)

NC Rennie Bere: The Nature of Cornwall (Barracuda Books, in association with the Cornwall Naturalists' Trust, 1982)

OCBS Charles Henderson and Henry Coates: Old Cornish Bridges and Streams (1928)

OWEMR J.H.Collins: Observations on the West of England Mining Region (1912, reprinted 1988)

PC Claude Berry: A Portrait of Cornwall (Hale, 1963; 3rd Edition, with additions by Donald R. Rawe, 1984)

PV	Bob Acton: The Landfall Book of the Poldice Valley (Landfall Publications, 1990)
Q&Q	Peter H. Stanier: Quarries and Quarrying (Shire, 1985)
RCR	D.B.Barton: The Redruth and Chasewater Railway, 1824-1915 (Bradford Barton, 1960)
T&TM	R.L.Atkinson: Tin and Tin Mining (Shire, 1985)
TEC	June Palmer: Truro in the Eighteenth Century (privately published, 1990)
TIA	R.D.Penhallurick: Tin in Antiquity(Institute of Metals,1986)
TKC	W.H.Pascoe: Teudar, A King of Cornwall (Truran, 1985)
TMSC	D.B.Barton: A History of Tin Mining and Smelting in Cornwall (Bradford Barton)
WG	Peter Stanier: The Work of Giants: Great Granite Rocks of Cornwall and Scilly (St Ives Printing & Publishing Company, 1988)

PLEASE NOTE The inclusion of a book in the above list does not necessarily mean that it is wholly reliable. Even the works of "authorities" like Collins, Dines, Hamilton Jenkin and Barton contain factual errors, as Kenneth Brown has demonstrated to me. A comforting thought to novices in the field like me!

The stepping stones at Penpol (Walk 11). The pile of old masonry beside the wooden post is a relic of the tide mill.

LANDFALL WALKS BOOKS:
ꞁRLIER VOLUMES IN THE SERIES

No Sev W FROM CARN MARTH, Pas amid Cornwall's Industrial (Sti **52 pages, price £2.50** ; available!)

No.2 BEA EW FROM ST AGNES Indu: it Walks amid Cornwall's price (1989) 68 pages, (Inclu stal footpath from Porthtowan to Ho hree inland walks. Like *Carn Marth* *Brea,* pays special attention to mining elated topics.)

No.3 Walks D THE FAL, Circular (Ten w **52 pages, price £2.70** d the Fal estuary, from Pendenn ılmouth, to St Mawes Castle, St Anth and Portscatho. Includes Trelissick le-known area around Ruan Lanihorn

No.4 HELFOR ID THE (1989, r ılar Walks revisions with slight price £2.9 64 pages, (Fourteen lve of them around the uary and two using the c path on the east side. A x very short walks are desc ief.)

No.5 ARC EWQUAY, Circular Walks froı ıthan to Holywell (1990) 64 p e £2.70 (Nine round of them covering the coastal footpat e inland, including the Vale of Lanher

No.6 A VIEW FROM CARN BREA, Circular Walks around Redruth, Camborne and Portreath (1990) 80 pages, price £2.95
(Twelve walks, three of which cover the coast path from Gwithian to Porthtowan. A sequel to No. 1, covering most of the northern and western parts of the Mineral Tramways route. Readers unfamiliar with the countryside around Camborne and Redruth will, I think, be surprised at the peacefulness and beauty of much of it, as well as the impressive industrial remains.)

No.7 AROUND THE RIVER FOWEY, Circular Walks (1990) 80 pages, price £2.95
(Twelve main walks and another twelve shorter ones. The Fowey estuary is the focal point, but the coast path from Polmear to Lansallos is covered, and there are inland walks including Lanhydrock, Restormel Castle, Lostwithiel, the Luxulyan Valley and Tywardreath, the setting of Daphne du Maurier's *The House on the Strand*)

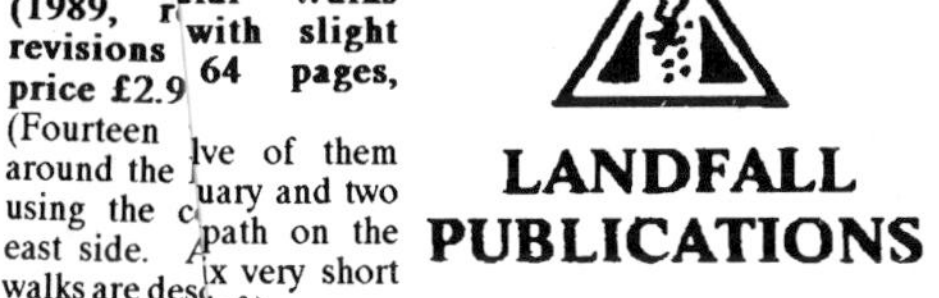

No.8 AROUND PADSTOW, Circular Walks from Porthcothan to Wadebridge and Bodmin (1991) 68 pages, price £3.30
(Ten main walks plus nine shorter ones based on the same routes. Each main walk makes use of one or more of the three long-distance paths that meet at Padstow: the South West Way (coast path), the Camel Trail and the Saints' Way. Like all the other books, it has detailed directions plus sketch maps, gives practical advice on parking, refreshments, etc., and is fully illustrated.)

ꞌER BOOKS BY BOB ACTON

THE LANDF OOK OF TRURO (1990) 16 page £1.25
(Handy street-ma ro plus a city-centre walk and four cou s starting and ending at the Cathedral.)

THE LANDFA OOK OF THE POLDICE VAL 1990) 72 pages including 8 in our, price £3.99
(Commissioned by t e Valley Trust and supported by a gı the Countryside Commission, this bo n some detail at the history of a district, just south of St Day, which for several decades was the world's main source of copper. The area is explored by means of a series of short, medium and longer walks and cycle rides; several of these again follow the Mineral Tramways Project routes. Sketch-maps, plans, drawings and photographs.)

TWELVE WALKS ON THE LIZARD (1989) 32 pages, price £1.75
(Available from the Tor Mark Press, Penryn.)

IN PREPARATION

Around Looe and Polperro
man's Cornwall": Port Isaac to Wadebridge
Around Mevagissey

A SELECTION OF REVIEWS OF OTHER LANDFALL BOOKS

Off the beaten track to an industrial past

A View from Carn Marth. Seven Walks Amid Cornwall's Industrial Past by Bob Acton (Landfall Publications, Penpol), £2.50.

TO STAND on the eastern peak of Carn Marth (757 feet) is to look out over the expanse of Cornwall, a rich coloured tapestry edged by English Channel and blue Atlantic.

Immediately below with the fields and even some woods, lie the scars of a former great mining industry. Some say this was once the richest mining area in the world.

The sun strikes Wheal Jane's steel headgear and miners still work deep underground at the veins of metal. On the surface, footpaths and country roads meander beside ruined engine houses, quiet wharves and "deads," where gorse and heather try to grow.

Not much of a place for the rambler or walker?

It certainly is, says Bob Acton, tracing circular walks that give a new insight into the area and industrial past and reveal some of its interesting and beautiful spots. (The West Briton, 27/4/89)

Jewel in the crown

Around the River Fowey, circular walks by Bob Acton, (Landfall Publications) £2.95.

BOB Acton's well-worn walking boots have now trudged the byways and footpaths around the river Fowey as he produces the seventh or his delightfully informative guides.

Well clear of West Cornwall, generally the setting for earlir circular walks, he moves into a gentle land, of sheltered creeks, wooded landscapes and wild flowers.

Here for everyone's delight is a four-mile walk along the beautiful Luxluyan Valley and through his pen in words and sketches, he waxes lyrical about this lovely way.

"When I get back from a walk like this the first thing I want to do is tell everyone about it," he writes. "But the impulse to keep it a closely guarded secret would be equally strong, were it not that it's already famous."

It certainly is a jewell but then so are many of the dozen walks and "Sunday afternoon specials", that he sets out step by step around the Fowey.

He not only lays out the route, but pinpoints in short articles and sketches places to be found along the walks of special note or history.

Just the size to slip into the back pocket, the book is worth its weight in gold with all its well researched information to turn an already pleasant walk into something rather special. JBB.

The West Briton 11/10/90

North Cornwall Advertiser, March 1991

Walks a plenty

If you are tramping out the walks of Cornwall one weekend and you happen upon a couple taking copious notes, or stopping to draw the scene, the chances are it will be Bob Acton and his wife.

Under his imprint of Landfall Publications - Bob has produced nine books so far, and not content with just writing and illustrating them himself, he also typesets them at home.

His latest is Around Padstow, which takes in circular walks from Porthcothan to Wadebridge and Bodmin. Landfall Walks Book No. 8.

Priced at a moderate £3.50,* it includes ten main walks ranging from three miles to seven, nine shorter walks based on the longer routes for the less energetic and a lot of the area's history, illustrated throughout.

Based on the Coastal Footpath, the Camel Trail and the Saints Way, Bob takes readers on walks into the "unchartered" countryside in this part of North Cornwall and, like a certain brew, reaches the parts that most other walks books do not.

Around the River Fowey, takes in Lostwithiel and the Luxulyn Valley, but more interesting to local people is Landfall Walks Book No. 5 entitled Around Newquay, which takes in nine circular walks from Bedruthan to Holywell Bay

Priced at £2.70 and produced in association with The Gallery of Old Newquay, the beauty of this book and the others in the series is the wealth of information which Bob gives his fellow walkers.

Bob thoroughly researches each walk and, unlike some walks books, caters for walkers' real needs by telling you where to get a snack, or have a wee! Now, that's just as important as knowing that the parish church is 13th century!

Like many people, however, Bob put off going to Newquay for quite some time "and until a few months ago had avoided it almost completely in the belief that the town is overcrowded all summer and ugly all year."

He proved himself wrong on both counts, and so can you with the help of this very informative book.

*Actually, an even more moderate £3.30!

How Bob turned a hobby into profession

WALKERS, historians and armchair discoverers all have the chance to, extend their activities following the publication of a new book last month.

"A View from Carn Brea" has been written by former teacher Bob Acton, who lives at Penpol near Truro.

His sixth publication, the book sets out a dozen routes for circular walks around Camborne, Redruth and Portreath, and describes a variety of points of interest to look out for along the way.

A keen walker himself, Bob decided to turn a hobby into a profession after taking early retirement.

He stated: "I hit on the idea of organising walking holidays as a way to bring in a bit of extra income, but I didn't get all that many enquiries.

"In the end I realised that I still had all the notes that I had made and so it seemed sensible to put them all in a book."

According to Bob the most enjoyable part of his work is the out-of-doors research.

"It is great fun meeting all the different people. I come across all sorts of old folks who have hun-

"Local people will fi[nd these] books useful and ins[tructive,] while tourists will find t[hem in]dispensable." (Ross Sal[...] The Sunday Independe[nt])

Call f[or] natio[nal] park

"Around the Fal C[...] by Bob Acton. Publi[c]ation with Cornish [...] fall Publications, Pe[...] £2.70.

WALKING enth[usiasts] have been cag[...] for this next [...] Acton will find i[t ...] as the rest.

His latest offe[rs ...] walks around the [...]ryside is filled [...] haunts to visit [...] information abo[ut ...] side of the vil[...] rounding area.

The book h[as ...] written and c[...] varied inform[...] enjoyable just [...] read.

The West B[riton ...]89

Co[...] ra[...]

"Around [...] Holy-[...]cular Walks from [...]ndfall well". by B[...] Publication [...] New-with The [...] quay). £2.7[0]

This is th[...] Land-[...]will be fall Walk[s ...] those warmly [...]hrough who enj[oy ...] and by coast an[d ...] previous readers [...] books.

It gi[...] of nine walks w[...] from two to t[...] shorter alt[...] the longer trated [...] illus-sketch[...]ings and

Bob [...] chatty notes about [...] and the past are a [...] read, whe-ther [...] at home or studi[...] away. JWB

The [West Brit]on, 11/10/90

[...] to tell [...]llage, but [...] the con-[...]ucation to [...]own," he [...]

[...] are already [...] the county, [...] have been [...] ex-patriots [...] the world.

[...]t book, with [...] history and [...]ps, is the ideal companion for [...] mental and [...]xplorer.

The Packet, 7/4/90

The Packet, 25/11/89

Bob reveal[s] hidden delights of Helford